CHARACTER

abeka.
Pensacola, FL 32523-9100
an affiliate of PENSACOLA CHRISTIAN COLLEGE®

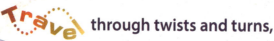

Travel through twists and turns, **ponder** plots and plays, and **connect** with an incredible cast as they get **IN CHARACTER.**

TO TEACHERS AND PARENTS

As students delve into *In Character*, they will meet lifetime literary friends in this compelling collection. A full cast of multidimensional and one-dimensional characters provide students the opportunity to study character development and authors' style. Selections include award-winning authors of classic literature such as Eleanor Estes, Jack Prelutsky, and Mary Mapes Dodge. Following each literary piece, thinking questions will challenge students to recall facts, analyze material, and draw valid conclusions while developing a biblical worldview.

Note: The Abeka Reading Program contains selections appropriate for each grade level, typifying specific literary genres written by a diverse range of authors. Selections have been carefully chosen to meet academic standards and to deepen students' understanding of literature. A selection's inclusion is based on literary merit and does not imply an endorsement of the author's worldview or of every work by the author. Throughout this anthology, students are guided to evaluate each selection through a biblical worldview as they encounter many true-to-life situations in literature.

In Character

Staff Credits
Managing Editor: Amy Yohe
Product Manager: Ximena Brainard
Edition Editors: Juliane Roberts, Rachel Grosnick, Dawn Mereness, Jennifer Odom, Ana Schriever
Contributors: Bethany Urbina, V. Valencia, Siera Weber
Designer: Ruth Ann Chappell
Cover Illustrator: Tim Uy
Illustrators: Brian Jekel, Jamieson Jekel, Tim Uy, Peter Kothe, Bobby Dalrymple, Jeremy Gorman, Joshua Burylo, Natasha Wodome, Abby Fabrizio

Credits appear on p. 282, which is considered an extension of copyright page.

Cataloging Data

       In character -- 1st ed.
   282 p. : col. ill. ; 22 cm
    1. Readers (Elementary) 2. Reading (Elementary)
III. Abeka Book, Inc.

Library of Congress: PE 1119 .I6 2024
Dewey System: 428.6

CONTENTS

(cont.)

Pronunciation Key

Symbol • Example		Symbol • Example	
ā	āte	ŏ	nŏt
â	dâre	oi	boil
ă	făt	o͞o	fo͞od
ä	fäther	o͝o	bo͝ok
ə	ago (ə·gō′)	ou	out
ē	ēven	th	thin
ĕ	ĕgg	t̶h̶	t̶h̶ere
ê (ər)	pondêr	t͞u̶	pict͞u̶re
ī	īce	ū	ūnit
ĭ	ĭt	û	hûrt
ō	ōver	ŭ	ŭp
ô	côrd, taught, saw	zh	measure

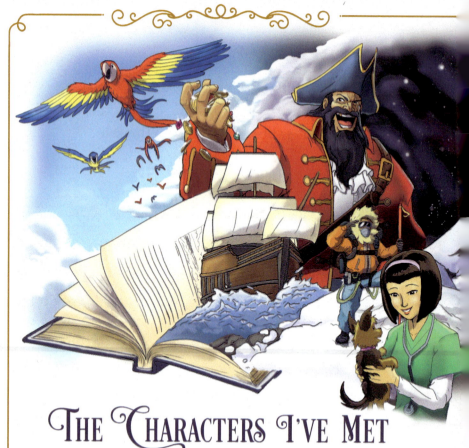

THE CHARACTERS I'VE MET

Siera Weber

One day I opened up a book.
The hero seized me by the hand.
Throughout the quest we undertook,
He taught me how to take a stand.

Another time, I turned the page
And met a villain vile and cruel.
His wicked deeds and evil rage
Taught me to treasure virtue's jewels.

In one book, I got to know
A friend whose choices brought defeat.
He learned from these, began to grow,
And soldiered on to vict'ry sweet.

Another story showed me how
To take on trials with a smile.
When life seems hard or painful now,
I still press on another mile.

Some characters that I have met
Were pierced by sorrow's painful darts.
Their sorrows soon became mine too.
Compassion's floods then filled my heart.

These characters have taught me things:
To love, to give, and to be kind.
I'll look for what the next book brings,
And characters that I will find.

◆ I W O N D E R . . .

1. What happens to the poet when she reads a book?

2. How do you think the author feels about books?

IN THE SPOTLIGHT

TITLE, AUTHOR, ❯ MAIN CHARACTER ❮

What is it about a particular book that makes you want to dive into it as it falls open? Maybe the cover art catches your eye immediately. Illustrations are important, but they can tell you only so much about the stories contained within the covers. Sometimes stories begin with a mysterious title that will draw you into the world of imagination. And sometimes it's the unforgettable characters that seem to come alive through creative descriptions. Exploring these and other parts of a story will open up an exciting new window into the world of reading.

The **title** is very important to the story. Often, a title tells exactly what the selection is about. Other times a title is chosen to spark interest or add mystery; its meaning becomes clear only after you have read the story. Also, somewhere on the book's cover or underneath the story's title, you will see the name of the **author**. The author, who is the writer of the story, understands the importance of the title because it is the first thing the reader notices about the selection. Paying close attention to titles and their meanings will help you choose a good one when it is time for you to write.

Characters come to
life when we understand
the selections we read. The
main character is *whom* the story is
mainly about. This character is the one that
does most of the action, most of the thinking, and
most of the talking. A character reflects specific moods
through his actions or behavior. Look for the traits that
describe the main character and that help the reader
understand the character's role. As you read, ask yourself,
"What does the main character say? How does he act?
How does he feel? How does he change from beginning
to end?"

An author uses an effective title and an interesting
main character to help make a story unique and engaging.
Understanding how the author uses them to fashion a
story will help you with your own writing and may also
help you choose the book you would like to dive into next.

 I   W O N D E R   .   .   .

1. What can the title do for a story?

2. Whom is the story mainly about?

3. What does the main character do in a story?

4. What are good questions to ask when analyzing a
   main character?

RUFUS
AND THE
FATAL FOUR
from *Rufus M.*
by Eleanor Estes

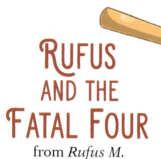

Times are hard for the Moffat family, as they are for all the families in Cranbury. Since America entered the Great War in Europe, everyone is making sacrifices. In spite of war abroad and hardships at home, Rufus, the youngest Moffat, is unstoppable. He has maneuvered his way into possessing his own library card, even though he is technically too young to have one. He solved the mystery of the invisible piano player, and he took a starring role the day his school marched to the train station to support the soldiers leaving for France. Now he has set his heart on joining the Fatal Four—whatever that may be. He hopes only that, somehow, punch and cookies will be involved.

Usually it made no difference whether or not Rufus was a left-handed person. In fact, now that the teacher had accepted this quirk[1] in Rufus's makeup, it was only awkward to be left-handed when somebody wanted to shake his right hand. So far no left-handed person had tried to shake hands with Rufus. Rufus hoped to meet one someday and then they would have a good left-handed shake.

But there was one occasion when it really was an asset[2] to be left-handed, Rufus found. And that was in connection with the Fatal Four.

---

[1] **quirk**—*uncommon trait*
[2] **asset**—*useful quality*

For some time Rufus had been seeing "The F. F." on all of Janey's notebooks and on the brown covers of her grammar and arithmetic books. He asked Jane what it meant. Jane said it was a secret. However, if Rufus would not tell anybody, the initials stood for the Fatal Four. More than that she would not say. Rufus assumed it had something to do with pirates. Therefore, he was really surprised when Jane, in a mood of confidence, further enlightened him to the extent of revealing that the Fatal Four was the name of a baseball team she belonged to that could beat anybody.

"Then," she went on to explain, "if the Fatal Four gets tired of baseball, oh, not gets tired 'cause they'll never do that, but if it should snow, and they couldn't play anymore, they'll still be the Fatal Four because it's a good name the members can keep always. Baseball . . . football . . . no matter what. Or it could just be a club to eat cookies and drink punch made out of jelly and water."

This all sounded good to Rufus, particularly the punch. He asked if he could join. Did it cost anything? Jane said she was sorry but the Fatal Four was all girls. However, she would try to bring him a cookie if they ever decided on punch and cookies instead of baseball. So for a time Rufus was not allowed to have anything to do with this team. But sometimes he went across the street to the big empty lot behind the library, sat down on a log, and watched them practice. There were a half-dozen or so silvery gray old telephone poles piled up in one part of the lot. Bleachers, Rufus called them, and that was where he sat to watch the Fatal Four.

Jane and Nancy had organized the Fatal Four baseball team. At first Jane was worried that they were playing baseball in October when the time for baseball is spring. She thought it would be better if the Fatal Four started right in with punch and cookies on Tuesdays. But once they had begun playing baseball she wondered how she could ever have been so foolish. She loved baseball and could not understand how anybody was happy who did not play it every day.

Naturally, since Jane and Nancy had thought up this whole team, there was no reason why they should not take the two most important roles, the pitcher and the catcher, for themselves. Jane was the catcher. She accepted this position because she thought the name alone would automatically make her a good one. "Yes," she said, "I'll be catcher." And she put her trust in the power of the title and the mitt to enable her to catch anything. Nancy was the pitcher. For a time they were the only members of the team, so they had to be the pitcher and the catcher, for in baseball that is the very least you can get along with. Soon, however, other girls in the neighborhood joined up.

"I'll be the captain," said Nancy. "Let's take a vote."

They took a vote and elected Nancy. Clara Pringle was the outfield to catch all flies. She never really had very much to do because there weren't many flies hit and she sat in the long grass and waited for business. A girl named Hattie Wood was first base. That made four girls they had on the team and that was when they decided to call themselves the Fatal Four.

So far Rufus had had nothing to do with this team except to sit and watch. He did this gladly, however, for he considered that anything that called itself the Fatal Four was worthy of being watched, especially if there was

6

that vague[3] possibility of pink punch and cookies in the offing.[4] He used to sit there pounding his fist into one of Joey's old mitts, hoping they'd take him into the Four.

At first the Fatal Four baseball team practiced ardently[5] every day. However, after a week or so Jane grew tired of chasing balls, since she rarely caught one. The mitt and the title of catcher had not produced the desired results.

"A backstop is what we need," she told Nancy.

None of the girls was willing to be a backstop. More-over, they were all needed where they were. Take Hattie Wood off first base and what kind of a team would they have? they asked themselves. An amateur team. The Fatal Four was anything but that, Nancy assured them. "But if you want a backstop, why not ask Rufus?" she suggested.

---

[3] **vague**—*not definite*
[4] **offing**—*near future*
[5] **ardently**—*enthusiastically*

Now there was much arguing back and forth as to whether or not they should invite Rufus to be the backstop. He was not a girl and this team was supposed to be composed of girls only. But then everybody thought how nice it would be to have Rufus chasing balls for them, so they enthusiastically assented.[6]

"After all," said Jane, "a backstop is not really part of the team. It's part of the grounds."

So that clinched it and that was how Rufus came to be backstop for the Fatal Four baseball team. Rufus was happy over the arrangement. When they abandoned baseball for punch and cookies, he might be an accepted member. Moreover, the more practice he had, the sooner the big boys would take him into their team, he thought. Certainly if the pitcher of the boys' baseball team had the same tendencies as Nancy, left-handed Rufus would be a tremendous asset.

Nancy used to be a rather good pitcher. But ever since the girls' baseball team had been organized, Nancy had taken to practicing curves. Somehow these curves always shot the ball way to the left of the batter. The batter would move farther and farther to the left, hoping to catch up with Nancy's curve balls. But it was no use. No matter how far to the left the batter edged, the farther to the left flew Nancy's pitches. Often the bases had to be moved several times during the game to catch up with the home plate. Frequently, by the end of the game, home plate was where the pitcher's box originally had been, and vice versa.[7] Nancy realized there was a flaw in her pitching which she would have to correct.

---

[6]**assented**—*agreed*

[7]**vice versa**—*in reversed order*

Meanwhile, it certainly was lucky the team now had a left-handed backstop, for Jane had a hard enough time catching just straight pitches, let alone these curve balls of Nancy's that veered[8] off to the left all the time. But Rufus had only to reach out his left arm farther and farther, and he caught most of them. What he didn't catch he cheerfully ran for, over Mr. Buckle's hen coop or in Mrs. Wood's asparagus patch that had gone to seed, or he hunted between the long silvery logs that lay lined up in a corner of the field.

As a reward for his backstop duties, Nancy pitched Rufus some curves, and since he was a left-handed batter, her pitches that veered to the left were just perfect for him and it was only when Rufus was at the bat that Clara Pringle, picking goldenrod in the outfield, had anything to do in the game.

This convinced Nancy that there was nothing wrong with her pitching after all. The trouble lay with the material she was working with. "Slug at 'em, fellas," she said. "Rufe hits 'em all." And the girls, feeling rather ashamed, now tried harder, sometimes even turning around and batting left-handed as Rufus did, hoping to hit Nancy's pitches.

One Saturday morning Rufus was sitting in the driver's seat of the old abandoned sleigh that was in the Moffats' barn. He was thinking that if he had a pony next winter he could harness it to this old sleigh and go for a ride. Suddenly Nancy and Janey burst around from the front yard. Nancy was swinging her bat. She had her pitcher's mitt on. Jane was pounding the baseball into Joey's big catcher's mitt, limbering[9] it up.

---

[8] **veered**—*turned off course*
[9] **limbering**—*making something flexible*

"Come on, Rufe," they yelled. "This is *the* day!"

"What! Punch and cookies?" exclaimed Rufus.

"No, we're having a real game today. Not just practice," they said.

For a long time Jane and Nancy had thought they were the only girls' baseball team in Cranbury, in the world in fact. Then one day a girl accosted[10] them after school. She said her name was Joyce Allen and that she was the captain of the Busy Bee baseball team, a team composed entirely of girls on the other side of town. She wanted to know whether or not Nancy, the captain of the F. F. team, would accept a challenge from her, the captain of the Busy Bee team, to play next Saturday. Nancy consulted Jane and said "Yes."

So now today was the day. Rufus climbed off the sleigh, found his old pitcher's mitt that he used to catch the curves, and they all marched across the street to the big lot behind the library where the game was going to be held. While they waited for the teams to show up, Rufus spit in his mitt, rubbed sand in it, and got it into condition to play.

"I hope we don't have to go all over town and round everybody up," said Jane impatiently.

The Fatal Four had added another team member, Nancy's sister, Beatrice, but they still called themselves the Fatal Four because it sounded better than fatal anything else. Since this team had such an excellent name, the F. F., it had plenty of applicants to join. Nancy and Jane were particular, however, saying to join the F. F. you really had to know something about baseball. Most applicants backed away apologetically when Nancy stated this firmly.

---

[10] **accosted**—*boldly confronted*

10

At last here came somebody across the lot. It was Joyce Allen, the captain of the Busy Bees.

"The others will be here soon," she said cheerfully. "Some of them hadn't finished washing the breakfast dishes, but they'll be here soon."

"While we're waitin'," said Jane, "since both the captains are here, we can see who's up at the bat first."

Rufus took the bat, threw it, and Nancy caught it. She put her right fist around the end of it, then the other captain put her fist above Nancy's and swiftly placing one fist above the other they measured the length of the bat. The visiting captain's left fist was the last one to fit the bat. It was a tight squeeze but fair, and  Rufus said that the visiting team was first up at the bat. Rufus sometimes had to act in the capacity[11] of umpire as well as backstop.

But where was the visiting team? Or Nancy's, for that matter?

Rufus began to feel impatient. Here were the captains. All right. Let the teams come then. "Why not have the punch instead?" he asked. But nobody paid any attention to him. It seemed to Rufus as though the game were off, and he decided, Fatal Four or no,

---

[11] **capacity**—*role; position*

to go and find something else to do. Over in a corner of the field some men had started to dig a cellar to a new house. This activity looked interesting to Rufus and he was about to investigate it when along came two girls, arms linked together. So Rufus stayed. There was always the possibility that the Fatal Four might switch from baseball to punch and cookies. Either was worth staying for in Rufus's opinion.

"These girls must be Busy Bees," said Nancy.

They *were* Busy Bees. They both admitted it. However, they said they wished they could join the F. F. instead. They liked the name of it. They had heard many rumors as to what it stood for. Most people thought it stood for Funny Fellows. Did it?

"Of course not!" said Nancy, and Jane clapped her hand over Rufus's mouth before he could say the Fatal Four and give away the secret. No matter what it stood for, the girls wanted to join it and be able to write the F. F. on all their red notebooks.

While the discussion was going on, three more girls arrived, three more Busy Bees. It seemed they, too, wanted to join the F. F., so they could write the F. F. on their notebooks also. Nancy and Jane looked at the captain. She must feel very badly at this desertion. But she didn't. She said she wished she could join the F. F., too.

"Oh, no," said Nancy. "You all better stay Busy Bees. What team would there be for us to beat if we let you join ours?"

So that settled the matter, and Busy Bees remained Busy Bees. Now they lined up at the home plate, for they were to be the first at the bat. At last the game began. *Thank goodness, Rufus is here behind me,* thought Jane, pounding her fist into the big catcher's mitt. For it really took two Moffats to make one good catcher. If one of them was she, that is.

Nancy's team did not get off to a good start. Nancy had been practicing her curve balls more than ever, and they swung more and more sharply to the left. If they had not had such a good left-handed backstop as Rufus, goodness knows where the balls would have landed. In order that they would not crash through a window of the library, the girls rearranged the bases many times.

Of course there was no danger of the balls crashing through the library windows from hits. The danger lay in the curves. So far she had not been able to strike the Busy Bees out. They were walking to base on balls. And the balls were flying wild now. Rufus had dashed across the lot to take a look at the men who were digging the cellar to the new house, and he was sorely missed. Jane, who had had enough trouble catching in the old days before Nancy cultivated her curve ball, was becoming desperate.

Right now happened to be a very tense moment. The captain of the Busy Bees was at the bat. There were men on all bases. They'd gotten there on walks. The captain had two strikes against her, however. She had been striking at anything, for she evidently had grown tired of just walking to base. If Nancy could strike her out, it would break the charm and maybe the Fatal Four team would have a chance at the bat. So far the Busy Bees had been at the bat the entire game. The score must be big. They had lost track of it.

Beside wanting to strike Captain Allen out, Nancy was trying especially hard to impress her. She came over to Jane and said in a low voice, "They'll think they have a better team than we have, and I bet that pitcher can't even throw curves! I've just got to strike her out!"

"Yes," agreed Jane, who was anxious to bat herself for a change.

"Watch for a certain signal," Nancy said. "When I hold my two middle fingers up, it means I'm going to throw a curve, a real one. It'll curve out there by the library, and then it will veer back, right plunk over the home plate. She won't strike at it because she'll think it's going over the library. But it won't, and she'll miss it and that's the way I'll put her out."

Jane nodded her head. Another curve! Of course curves made it real baseball and not amateur. She knew that much. All the same she wished she had said, "Why don't you pitch 'em straight for a change?" But she didn't have the courage. Nancy was the captain and the pitcher. She certainly should know how to pitch if she was the pitcher. Nancy wasn't telling Jane how to catch. She expected Jane to know how to catch since she was the catcher. She didn't tell her anything. So neither did Jane tell Nancy anything, and she waited for the signal and wished that Rufus would return and backstop for this very important pitch.

Now Nancy was winding her arm around and around. Then she stopped. She held up her middle two fingers. The signal! Jane edged over to the left but Nancy frowned her back. Oh, of course. This curve was really going to fly over home plate. Nancy crooked her wrist and threw! The girl at the bat just dropped to the ground when she saw the ball coming and she let it go. And the ball really did come right over home plate only it was way up in the air, way, way up in the air and spinning swiftly

toward the library window, for it did its veering later than calculated. Jane leaped in the air in an effort to catch it but she missed.

"Rufus! Rufus!" she yelled, and she closed her eyes and stuck her fingers in her ears, waiting for the crash.

Just in the nick of time Rufus jumped for the ball. He caught it in his left hand before it could crash through the window. He sprinted over with the ball.

"We'd better move the bases again," said Nancy. And they all moved farther away from the library.

"Stay here," said Jane to Rufus, pleadingly. So Rufus stayed and he said since he had caught the ball the girl was out, and why not have punch now? Jane gave him a nudge. This was real baseball and he mustn't think about anything else. The girl said it didn't count that Rufus caught the ball, for he was the backstop and not on the team. Even so, she graciously permitted Nancy's team a turn at the bat now, because the Busy Bees had had a long enough inning. They had run up such a big score she was sure the F. F. could never come up to it.

That's the way with baseball, thought Jane. *Whoever is first at the bat usually wins.*

Nancy was the first one up of the Fatal Four. The captain of the Busy Bee baseball team did not throw curves. Nancy struck at the first ball. It was a hit. She easily made first base. Now Jane was at the bat. Rufus, who decided to play backstop for the foreign team as well as Jane's, was pounding his fist into his mitt to get some real atmosphere[12] into this game.

While the pitcher was winding her arm around and around, Jane was busy, too. She was swinging the bat, limbering up. At last, she thought. At last she was at the bat. That's all she liked to do in baseball. Bat! And so far she hadn't had a chance. And she swung herself completely around in her enthusiasm. Unfortunately the bat flew out of her hand and it hit Rufus on the forehead.

Rufus was staggered and saw stars. However, he tossed it off saying, "Aw, it didn't hurt," even though a lump began to show. Jane rubbed his forehead, and thereafter she swung with more restraint. Even so, the catcher and Rufus automatically stepped back a few paces whenever Jane was at the bat, taking no chances with another wallop.

But now the pitcher pitched. Jane, still subdued[13] and repressed,[14] merely held the bat before her. Bang! The

---

[12] **atmosphere**—*mood or feeling*
[13] **subdued**—*controlled*
[14] **repressed**—*holding back; restrained*

16

ball just came up and hit it and rolled halfway toward the pitcher. Both the pitcher and the catcher thought the other was going to run for the ball. Therefore, neither one ran, and Jane made first base easily, putting Nancy on second. Now the bases were full because that's all the bases they had. And it was Clara Pringle at the bat.

The situation was too grave[15] for Clara. She did not want to bat. How could she ever face Nancy if she struck out? Nancy and Jane might never speak to her again if she struck out. Besides, she had hurt her wrist pulling up a stubborn pie-weed when she was in outfield. She looked at Jane, who was dancing toward second, and Nancy, who was dancing toward home, impatiently waiting for the hit that would send them in. Clara gulped at her position of unexpected responsibility. When she joined the Fatal Four she had never envisioned[16] being in a spot like this. She raised her hand to make a request.

"Can Rufus pinch-hit for me because I hurt my wrist?" she asked timidly.

Rufus did not wait for anybody to say yes or no. He threw his mitt at Clara and seized the bat, pounding the ground, the home plate, and an old bottle. That's the way he warmed up, and if Jane had been vociferous[17] at the bat, Rufus was nothing short of a tornado.

"Stand still!" yelled the pitcher. "You make me dizzy."

Rufus swung at imaginary balls.

"Hey!" exclaimed the pitcher. "He's left-handed."

"Sure," said Jane. "Why not?"

---

[15] **grave**—*serious*
[16] **envisioned**—*imagined*
[17] **vociferous**—*characterized by noise and excitement*

"You call 'em southpaws," said Nancy. "I pitch good to him myself."

"Well, here goes," said the pitcher. "It just looks funny if you're not used to 'em." And she swung her arm around and around again.

While she was warming up and while Rufus was stomping around, swinging the bat, waiting for the ball, Spec Cullom, the iceman, came along Elm Street. Evidently he saw in an instant that this was a real game and not just practice, for he stopped his team, threw down the iron weight to anchor his horse, Charlie, and strode into the lot and straddled the nearest log in the bleachers to watch. Rufus saw him and became even more animated with the bat.

At the same moment the twelve o'clock whistle blew. Now all the children were supposed to go home to lunch. The Busy Bees were in favor of stopping, but the Fatal Four protested. Here they were with all bases full and they should certainly play the inning out at least.

So the pitcher pitched and Rufus struck. Crack! He hit the ball! Up and up it sailed, trailing the black tape it was wound with behind it like the tail of a kite!

As it disappeared from sight in the pine grove, Nancy ran to home plate and Jane ran to second base, and then home, and Rufus tore to first, and then to second and then home. And so it was a home run that had been hit.

"A home run!" everybody yelled in excitement. It was surprising that that hit had not broken a window, and the outfielder of the visiting team ran in search of the ball. But she couldn't find it and Clara joined her, for she was an experienced outfielder, but she couldn't find it, either. Then the whole Busy Bee baseball team ran and looked for the ball, but they couldn't find it. So they all went home. The captain, impressed by the home run, yelled to Nancy that the score must have been a tie and they'd come back in a week or so to see who was the champ.

Jane and Nancy ran over to the pine grove to look for the ball. They hunted in the corner of the lot where skunk cabbage grew thick and melon vines covered a dump, covered even the sign that said DO NOT DUMP. They searched through the long field grass on this side of the library, trying not to get the thick bubbly-looking dew on their bare legs. Was this really snake spit as Joey and Rufus claimed? Jane wondered. If it was, where were all the snakes? She'd never seen a single snake. But where was the ball? That was some home run!

"You don't suppose he batted it clear across Elm Street into that lot, do you?" asked Nancy incredulously.[18]

"Might have," said Jane, not knowing whether to be proud or ashamed. And the two girls crossed the street to take a look, just in case Rufus had swung as mighty an arm as that.

---

[18] incredulously—*doubtfully*

Rufus did not join in the search. He ran around from base to base to home plate, again and again, in ever-widening circles until his course led him to the iceman. The iceman was one of his favorite people in Cranbury.

"Here," said Spec, "catch." And he threw the missing baseball to Rufus. "I yelled to the team that I caught the ball, but they couldn't hear me, I guess, what with whistles blowing and all the cheers. Some batter!" he said. "Keep it up, fella, and maybe next spring you can be batboy for the South End baseball team."

Having earned his place as one of the Fatal Four, Rufus now sets his sights on new worlds to conquer. He re-doubles his support for the war effort by planting a Victory Garden. But will those beans ever have the chance to grow? Will the washcloth he made as part of a class project ever make it to France and into the hands of a soldier? Rufus, stalwart and unfazed, perseveres on the home front. Whether he attempts to master the art of ventrilo-quism or takes a forbidden trip alone to The Great White Way, Rufus is ready for a challenge. An adventure awaits on every page of *Rufus M.*, a 1944 Newbery Honor Book.

Time to Think

1. What was the Fatal Four? BasBall

2. What was wrong with Nancy's pitching? her hand was low

3. What was Rufus's job? Back up Player

4. What did Rufus finally get to do at the end that he had wanted to do all along?
   Play BesBall

20

❖ I WONDER . . .

1. In what children's classic do we find the excerpt "Rufus and the Fatal Four"?

2. Who is the author of this award-winning book?

3. Why do you think the title "Rufus and the Fatal Four" was chosen for this chapter?

4. Who is the main character?

5. If Rufus's name had not been in the title, how would you know that he is the main character?

6. How might the story be different if Janey were the main character?

1. good
2. h
3. Because Rufus got in the team
4. Rufus Nancy
5.
6.

To focus on Main Character, see page 270.

IN THE SPOTLIGHT

❧ PLOT AND SETTING ☙

The **plot** is the sequence of events in a story, or the events that make up the beginning, middle, and ending. Sometimes the plot is called the story line. A skillful author will write a plot with events that build interest and excitement until it reaches its most exciting point. This point in the story line is called the **climax**, or the turning point of the story. At the climax, the characters' actions change, events suddenly change, or surprises are revealed. After the climax, the story's events start to slow down, problems start to be resolved, and solutions are reached as the story concludes. In the selection "Rufus and the Fatal Four," the climax occurs when Rufus comes to bat. The bases are loaded, and the opposing pitcher is not anticipating a left-handed batter! After Rufus hits a home run, the story quickly winds down to a happy conclusion.

When and where the story takes place is the story's **setting**. The author creates the setting for a story just as an artist creates the background for a portrait. The story's setting gives the reader a framework in which the events of the plot play out. It helps the reader make sense of what he sees, hears, and feels surrounding the characters in the plot. Look for clues to discover

whether the story
could have happened
today, long ago, or only in the
imagination. Other clues from the author
fill you in on the location of the story's events.
The setting of "Rufus and the Fatal Four" is in the small town of Cranbury around the time of World War I. It is October, and although baseball is out of season, Janey and Nancy have decided to form a team. The author adds realism to the setting by having one of the Fatal Four sit in the outfield and pick goldenrod—an autumn flower.

The action of the story line and the background against which it plays out are key elements in creating an interesting and original narrative. As you write, try to find ways to use time and place, plus action, to give your story depth and believability.

✦ I WONDER . . .

1. Events that make up the story line are part of the _____.
    a. plot   b. setting

2. What might the reader expect to happen at the climax?

3. Which of these questions describes the setting?
    a. What?   c. Where?
    b. When?   d. Who?

4. Descriptions of what the characters see, hear, and feel are part of the _____.
    a. plot   b. setting

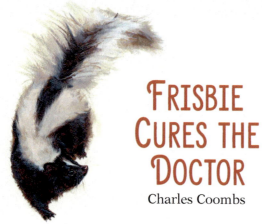

FRISBIE CURES THE DOCTOR

Charles Coombs

Lem and his pet skunk Frisbie are known by just about everyone in town. Lem is concerned about Frisbie and decides to bring him to see Doctor Boland, the town's veterinarian. The doctor is not one of Frisbie's admirers, but he reluctantly agrees to take a look at the skunk. The doctor may be able to cure Frisbie, but how will Frisbie cure the doctor?

Lem Burgin is usually as cheerful as a cat in a salmon cannery.[1] But on that particular morning, when he came to the back door in answer to my call, I could see trouble written all over his freckled face.

"Lem," I said, "it can't be that bad."

"It—it's Frisbie," he said solemnly.

"You mean he has disappeared? Run away?" I'm afraid I wasn't very careful at hiding the hope in my voice.

"Frisbie is ill," Lem explained.

"And I suppose you walked the floor all night with a sick skunk," I scoffed.

"It might be serious, Ned," he said. "Come on in and have a look at him."

"You've got him in the house?"

---

[1] **cannery**—*a factory where meat, fruit, and vegetables are placed in cans*

"Why not?"

"Thanks, but I think I'll stay out here where a guy has a fifty-fifty chance of making a clean break, should Frisbie become incensed[2] at something."

"Have it your way," Lem said. "But someday you'll learn to appreciate Frisbie."

"Don't hold your breath. On second thought, it's a good idea, when you're around Frisbie."

Lem went back into the house, letting my humor pass unheeded. Quickly he came back carrying an apple box. I eased cautiously to windward as Lem set the box on the lawn.

"Come on, Ned," Lem said impatiently. "He's not going to bite you!"

"Look, pal, I've never been worried about Frisbie biting me."

I moved in closer, then. I wasn't really as afraid of Frisbie as I let on. After all, we had been through quite a few adventures together, Lem, Frisbie, and I. And, as yet, neither Lem nor I had had to bury any clothes. Still, I never wanted to be caught off guard.

Well, Frisbie did look somewhat peaked, at that. He turned his shoe-button eyes

---

[2] **incensed**—*enraged; extremely angry*

up toward us. His teeth were making a sort of clicking sound. I'll admit I was somewhat moved by the poor little fellow's sad appearance.

"Skunk fever," I said professionally.

"No, I think he has a sticker in his ear," Lem corrected. "Notice how he holds his head over to one side. See the swelling? Look close, Ned."

Well, maybe I was moved, but not that close.

"We've got to take him to a doctor," Lem said.

"A doctor! Lem, you're the guy to take to a doctor, if you think anyone would let you within a block of his office with Frisbie."

"There's Doctor Boland down on Cypress Street. He's a veterinarian."

"Cats and dogs," I reminded him.

"A good veterinarian should know about all animals."

"Even skunks?"

"Skunks are animals. Come on. That sticker or whatever it is may be working its way toward Frisbie's brain!"

"Skunks don't need brains," I said, but I fell in beside him as he started toward town. "You know, Lem, Doc Boland has the reputation of being very high priced, even for treating far less complicated animals."

But Lem's sense of economy was blinded by his love for Frisbie. He didn't answer.

We arrived at the white stucco³ building which housed Doc Boland's dog-and-cat hospital. The barking of dogs and the meowing of cats filtered through the partition⁴ that separated the waiting room from the rest

---

³ **stucco**—*thick plaster used for covering outside walls*
⁴ **partition**—*a thin wall that divides a room into sections*

of the building. We waited and made sufficient noise to attract anyone's attention who might be in the back room. Still, no one showed up.

"Bolands live in a house in the rear," I said. "Maybe the doctor's eating lunch. Let's go see."

We found him back there, all right. He was an elderly man, not given much to smiling. He had a fringe of white hair that formed a windbreak around a patch of arid[5] scalp. He peered out at us over his bifocals.[6]

"What's on your minds, boys?" he said. "If you had gone into the office, I'd have known you were here."

"We did go inside," I said.

"You did? Then that buzzer must be out of order again." He pointed to the wire that ran back from the hospital and disappeared into a small square box under the porch eaves. "Well, anyway—here, Myra," he spoke to the cute little three- or four-year-old girl who had been sitting on his lap, "you'd better get down now so I can see what these boys want. My granddaughter," he explained proudly.

"She sure is cute," I said, cootcheecooing her under the chin, then watching her run pell-mell[7] around the house. Always good business to get in solid with the kids, I thought. Might help Lem when the bills were written.

"I—I have a sick animal here, Doctor Boland." Lem suddenly came to life.

"Well, you've come to the right place. Must be a small one. Let's have a look in that box, and—whoa! Hey, what kind of a joke—get that thing out of here!"

---

[5] **arid**—extremely dry
[6] **bifocals**—eyeglass lenses that have one section for near vision and another section for distant vision
[7] **pell-mell**—in a frantic, hasty manner

Well, I think Lem could have stood anything but to have a man whose profession is animals take such a sudden offense at Frisbie. The look of disillusionment[8] that cast a cloud over Lem's face was pretty awful to behold. As for me, I was never one to defend Frisbie. In fact, Frisbie had never needed help. But this was different, somehow.

"Lem's skunk is friendly and tame, Doctor Boland," I said quickly, quite astounded at the sound of my own words. "And he's ill. Even a sick skunk deserves some sort of care."

"Not by me." Doctor Boland stood adamant[9] with his back to the wall. "Take him to the dog pound or the city incinerator,[10] or—"

That was dangerous talk for anybody, with Lem around. And the very fact that he didn't challenge Doctor Boland's thoughtless remark convinced me of just how concerned Lem was over Frisbie's health.

"I—I'll pay you whatever you ask," Lem said in a sort of choking voice.

Well, a tasty carrot like that dangling before his nose was more than even Doctor Boland could seem to ignore. He began to breathe somewhat more easily, and I could almost hear the adding machine in his mind making mental calculations.

"All right, if you guarantee that he's harmless. What seems to be the trouble?"

"I think he has a sticker or something in his ear," Lem explained.

Doctor Boland moved slowly closer, but kept his hands well to himself. "Sort of looks like it, at that. All right,

---

[8] disillusionment—*giving up on expectations that have not come to pass*
[9] adamant—*unwilling to yield or change one's opinion or position*
[10] incinerator—*a furnace used to burn trash*

bring him into the hospital. We'll give him some anesthetic[11] and see what we can find."

"Anesthetic?"

"Of course. I wouldn't touch him without putting him to sleep first. We do it most of the time with any animal."

Lem seemed to accept it philosophically.[12] He even held Frisbie, while Doctor Boland applied the saturated cloth over Frisbie's tiny black nose. First the sweat broke out on Lem's forehead; then he got pale. For a minute I thought he was going to faint.

"There it is," Doctor Boland said, laying down a long pair of tweezers which were grasped around a long foxtail-like sticker. "Quite a bit of infection in there, but this penicillin will straighten it up in a hurry. You'd better get your friend a drink of water," he said to me. "You'll find a water cooler down the hallway. Don't get near those dog cages. There are two or three mean ones."

Well, he didn't have to tell me twice. As I went down the middle of the corridor, a couple of big mutts lunged at the wire as though nothing would make them happier than to tear me limb from limb.

Lem was gulping the water when the phone rang. Doctor Boland soon returned. "I have to go pick up a dog down on Elm Street," he said. "You might as well ride over with me. That animal will be some time coming out of the anesthetic. The fresh air will do you good. Especially you, young fellow," he indicated Lem, who was still rubbery in the legs. Lem seemed unwilling to leave Frisbie.

"Come on, Lem," I prompted. "He'll be okay."

---

[11] **anesthetic**—*a medicinal substance that numbs pain*
[12] **philosophically**—*relying on reason and wisdom*

Doctor Boland changed the cardboard clock in the door window to *Back in 10 Minutes,* and we were soon headed for Elm Street to pick up a fancy mutt that needed a bath.

Having had some difficulty in locating the little Pekingese[13] which had hidden in a closet at the very mention of a bath, it was somewhat after ten minutes when we returned to the dog-and-cat hospital. On the way back, Doctor Boland had hinted of various and sundry[14] charges for anesthesia (imagine having to gas a skunk!), penicillin, professional services rendered, to say nothing of what he called extraordinary expenses. I could see that he was planning to clear up whatever mortgages might be hanging over his head. It was going to be a sad time for Lem, on a fifty-cents a week allowance.

We went on in the door. And the minute we stepped inside, I had one of those unexplainable feelings that something was wrong. There seemed to be more noise coming from the animals beyond the office partition. The inner door was ajar.

And suddenly from beyond it came the unmistakable crying of a child. The sound froze us momentarily in our tracks. I say "us," but I think it was Doctor Boland's sudden stiffening, as he dropped the Pekingese to the floor.

"Myra!" he gasped. And I remembered that Myra was his granddaughter. I also knew intuitively[15] that Myra was not allowed in the dog-and-cat hospital.

Ordinarily, it might not have been such a startling situation. But the throaty growling of a dog sifted through

---

[13] **Pekingese** (pē′kə·nēz)—*a small dog with a flat nose, long hair, and a tail that curls over its back*
[14] **sundry**—*assorted; not all the same*
[15] **intuitively**—*immediately knowing how to respond based on instinct*

the many sounds. That growling did not come from the area of the heavy wire kennels. One of the dogs was out.

And, from the sound, it was one of the mean ones.

Lem went through the door, with me right at his heels and Doctor Boland crowding close behind.

What we saw was enough to make anyone turn and run. Right in the doorway that led to the kennels stood a large, wild-eyed dog. His teeth were bared. He lunged, then jumped back; he lowered his head and swayed this way and that.

"Grampa! Grampa!" The little girl was crowded back into a corner of the small operating room opposite the doorway to the kennels.

On the floor between her and the doorway which framed the drooling dog stood a small black-and-white furry object. His tiny teeth clicked angrily as he held the large animal at bay.[16]

"Frisbie!" Lem said, but he didn't move to pick up his pet. Frisbie seemed to have things well under control.

Doctor Boland hurried the girl out into the waiting room and closed the door. "Give me that chair," he said,

---

[16] **at bay**—*cornered while being challenged*

and I could tell that he was having trouble with his voice. The realization of what that dog might have done to his granddaughter was enough to make us all lose our voices.

I slid the chair over to him, and he moved in toward the dog, relieving Frisbie of his vigil.[17]

The dog wasn't mad; he was just mean. But Doctor Boland knew how to handle him.

Then he came back and sat down heavily. The sweat was pouring off his forehead. "We—we've told her a hundred times not to come back here," he explained.

"Kids will be kids," I said.

"There should be padlocks on those kennel doors," Lem said.

"There will be," Doctor Boland said. "There will be!"

Well, there was no sense in anyone bawling out anyone. It was one of those things that could have been very, very serious—had it not been for a certain little fellow who wasn't afraid to stand up to anything or anyone.

"It's well that—Frisbie came out of the anesthetic in time," Doctor Boland said. "Son, if that animal ever needs any attention of any kind, bring him to me."

"He could probably use an occasional bath," I put in helpfully, and the doctor never batted an eye.

Funny thing, too, Lem never did receive a bill from Doctor Boland. And he can't figure out why every once in a while there's a case of dog-and-cat food left on his doorstep.

"But, Ned," he says, "I didn't order any dog-and-cat food."

"Frisbie likes it, doesn't he?"

---

[17] **vigil**—*a time of waiting and watching*

Ellie

"Likes it? And how!"

"Then stop worrying." I say, "Frisbie ordered it, and he paid for it in full."

Time to Think

1. Why was Ned afraid to get close to Frisbie?

2. What finally convinced Dr. Boland to help Frisbie?

3. What did Frisbie do that proved his worth?

4. How did Doctor Boland's attitude toward the skunk change from the beginning of the story to the end of the story?

I WONDER . . .

1. Why do you think the title of this story is "Frisbie Cures the Doctor" instead of "The Doctor Cures Frisbie"?

2. Sequence the plot by numbering the following events in order.

   1 Lem and Ned arrive at the vet's office.

   2 Lem thinks Frisbie has a sticker in his ear.

   5 Cases of dog-and-cat food mysteriously appear on Lem's porch.

   3 Dr. Boland removes the sticker from Frisbie's ear.

   6 A mean dog corners Myra, and Frisbie keeps it at bay.

   7 Lem never gets a bill for the doctor's services.

   4 The boys ride along with the doctor to pick up a dog while they wait for Frisbie to recover.

3. What was the climax of this selection?

4. What is the story's setting?

IN THE SPOTLIGHT

❧ SUMMARIZATION ☙

Every story, play, or poem can be **summarized** in a short phrase or sentence. To summarize the story, condense the plot to its most basic elements. You should leave out many of the story's details, although you could include the name of the main character.

Your summary should be specific to the selection. For example, you have probably read many stories about pets, but the word *pets* would not summarize a story because it is not specific to the story. The selection "Frisbie Cures the Doctor" is about a pet skunk, but the phrase *pet skunk* does not summarize the story because it tells nothing about the story's plot. However, a sentence like this expresses what the story is mainly about: *Frisbie the skunk proves to be an unlikely hero and earns the gratitude of all.* It does not tell all the details; it just sums up the story.

Think about this sentence summarizing the plot of "Rufus and the Fatal Four": *The youngest Moffat, left-handed Rufus, is determined to become part of the team known as the Fatal Four.* Does it tell you the main idea of the story? There is not too much information, but we have learned who the main character is and what the story line is about.

 ## Time to Think

1. What would you include when summarizing a plot?
   a. many of the story's details
   b. most basic elements of the plot
   c. name of the main character
2. Summarize "The Characters I've Met" on page 1.

MORAL

In every story, the reader can expect to find characters, plot, and setting; however, not all literary works have a moral, depending on the author's purpose. Some stories are written simply for readers to enjoy; but if the author wants to teach a lesson, he will include a **moral**. The moral of the story is the lesson that the author hopes the reader will learn. Within the plot, the characters may experience effects brought about by a **cause**. These **effects** may produce a **problem** that needs to be **solved**. See how many of these elements you can find in this next selection.

THE PETERKINS SNOWED-UP

from *The Peterkin Papers* by Lucretia P. Hale

The Peterkins are a loving and humorous family of the 1800s, but they lack one important thing—common sense. For the Peterkins, tiny problems can become big catastrophes because they fail to find the simplest solutions. When a heavy snowstorm traps the family indoors, the Peterkins must put their unique problem-solving skills to the test.

Mrs. Peterkin awoke one morning to find a heavy snow-storm raging. The wind had flung the snow against the windows, had heaped it up around the

35

house, and thrown it into huge white drifts over the
fields, covering hedges and fences.

Mrs. Peterkin went from one window to the other
to look out; but nothing could be seen but the driving
storm and the deep white snow. Even Mr. Bromwick's
house, on the opposite side of the street, was hidden by
the swift-falling flakes.

"What shall I do about it?" thought Mrs. Peterkin.
"No roads cleared out! Of course there'll be no butcher
and no milkman!"

The first thing to be done was to wake up all the
family early; for there was enough in the house for
breakfast, and there was no knowing when they would
have anything more to eat.

It was best to secure the breakfast first.

So she went from one room to the other, as soon as
it was light, waking the family, and before long all were
dressed and downstairs.

All the water-pipes that there were were frozen. The
milk was frozen. They could open the door into the

wood-house; but the wood-house door into the yard was banked up with snow; and the front door, and the piazza[1] door, and the side door stuck. Nobody could get in or out!

Meanwhile, Amanda, the cook, had succeeded in making the kitchen fire, but had discovered there was no furnace coal.

"The furnace coal was to have come to-day," said Mrs. Peterkin, apologetically.

"Nothing will come to-day," said Mr. Peterkin, shivering.

But a fire could be made in a stove in the dining-room. All were glad to sit down to breakfast and hot coffee. The little boys were much pleased to have "ice-cream" for breakfast.

"When we get a little warm," said Mr. Peterkin, "we will consider what is to be done."

"I am thankful I ordered the sausages yesterday," said Mrs. Peterkin. "I was to have had a leg of mutton to-day."

"Nothing will come to-day," said Agamemnon,[2] gloomily.

"Are these sausages the last meat in the house?" asked Mr. Peterkin.

"Yes," said Mrs. Peterkin.

The potatoes also were gone, the barrel of apples empty, and she had meant to order more flour that very day.

"Then we are eating our last provisions," said Solomon John, helping himself to another sausage.

"I almost wish we had stayed in bed," said Agamemnon.

"I thought it best to make sure of our breakfast first," repeated Mrs. Peterkin.

---

[1] **piazza**—*a partially enclosed porch*

[2] **Agamemnon** (ăg′ə·mĕm′nŏn)—*the character named after a distinguished mythological Greek king*

"Shall we literally have nothing left to eat?" asked Mr. Peterkin.

"There's the pig!" suggested Solomon John.

Yes, happily, the pigsty was at the end of the wood-house, and could be reached under cover. But some of the family could not eat fresh pork.

"We should have to corn[3] part of him," said Agamemnon.

"My butcher has always told me," said Mrs. Peterkin, "that if I wanted a ham I must keep a pig. Now we have the pig, but have not the ham!"

"Perhaps we could 'corn' one or two of his legs," suggested one of the little boys.

"We need not settle that now," said Mr. Peterkin. "At least the pig will keep us from starving."

The little boys looked serious; they were fond of their pig.

"If we had only decided to keep a cow," said Mrs. Peterkin.

"Alas! yes," said Mr. Peterkin, "one learns a great many things too late!"

"Then we might have had ice-cream all the time!" exclaimed the little boys.

Indeed, the little boys, in spite of the prospect of starving, were quite pleasantly excited at the idea of being snowed-up, and hurried through their breakfasts that they might go and try to shovel out a path from one of the doors.

"I ought to know more about the water-pipes," said Mr. Peterkin. "Now, I shut off the water last night in the bath-room, or else I forgot to; and I ought to have shut it off in the cellar."

---

[3] **corn**—*to preserve in salt and water*

The little boys came back. Such a wind at the front door, they were going to try the side door.

"Another thing I have learned to-day," said Mr. Peterkin, "is not to have all the doors on one side of the house, because the storm blows the snow against *all* the doors."

Solomon John started up.

"Let us see if we are blocked up on the east side of the house!" he exclaimed.

"Of what use," asked Mr. Peterkin, "since we have no door on the east side?"

"We could cut one," said Solomon John.

"Yes, we could cut a door," exclaimed Agamemnon.

"But how can we tell whether there is any snow there?" asked Elizabeth Eliza,—"for there is no window."

In fact, the east side of the Peterkins' house formed a blank wall. The owner had originally planned a little block of semi-detached houses. He had completed only one, very semi and very detached.

"It is not necessary to see," said Agamemnon, profoundly; "of course, if the storm blows against this side of the house, the house itself must keep the snow from the other side."

"Yes," said Solomon John, "there must be a space clear of snow on the east side of the house, and if we could open a way to that"—

"We could open a way to the butcher," said Mr. Peterkin, promptly.

Agamemnon went for his pickaxe. He had kept one in the house ever since the adventure of the dumb-waiter.[4]

"What part of the wall had we better attack?" asked Mr. Peterkin.

---

[4] **dumb-waiter**—*a small elevator used for transporting food and other items*

Mrs. Peterkin was alarmed.

"What will Mr. Mudge, the owner of the house, think of it?" she exclaimed. "Have we a right to injure the wall of the house?"

"It is right to preserve ourselves from starving," said Mr. Peterkin. "The drowning man must snatch at a straw!"

"It is better that he should find his house chopped a little when the thaw comes," said Elizabeth Eliza, "than that he should find us lying about the house, dead of hunger, upon the floor."

Mrs. Peterkin was partially convinced.

The little boys came in to warm their hands. They had not succeeded in opening the side door, and were planning trying to open the door from the wood-house to the garden.

"That would be of no use," said Mrs. Peterkin, "the butcher cannot get into the garden."

"But we might shovel off the snow," suggested one of the little boys, "and dig down to some of last year's onions."

Meanwhile, Mr. Peterkin, Agamemnon, and Solomon John had been bringing together their carpenter's tools, and Elizabeth Eliza proposed using a gouge,[5] if they would choose the right spot to begin.

The little boys were delighted with the plan, and hastened to find,—one, a little hatchet, and the other a gimlet.[6] Even Amanda armed herself with a poker.

"It would be better to begin on the ground floor," said Mr. Peterkin.

"Except that we may meet with a stone foundation," said Solomon John.

[5] **gouge**—*a hand tool used to carve wood*
[6] **gimlet**—*a hand tool used for boring holes*

"If the wall is thinner upstairs," said Agamemnon, "it will do as well to cut a window as a door, and haul up anything the butcher may bring below in his cart."

Everybody began to pound a little on the wall to find a favorable place, and there was a great deal of noise. The little boys actually cut a bit out of the plastering with their hatchet and gimlet. Solomon John confided to Elizabeth Eliza that it reminded him of stories of prisoners who cut themselves free, through stone walls, after days and days of secret labor.

Mrs. Peterkin, even, had come with a pair of tongs in her hand. She was interrupted by a voice behind her.

"Here's your leg of mutton, marm!"

It was the butcher. How had he got in?

"Excuse me, marm, for coming in at the side door, but the back gate is kinder blocked up. You were making such a pounding I could not make anybody hear me knock at the side door."

"But how did you make a path to the door?" asked Mr. Peterkin. "You must have been working at it a long time. It must be near noon now."

"I'm about on regular time," answered the butcher. "The town team has cleared out the high road, and the wind has been down the last half-hour. The storm is over."

True enough! The Peterkins had been so busy inside the house they had not noticed the ceasing of the storm outside.

"And we were all up an hour earlier than usual," said Mr. Peterkin, when the butcher left. He had not explained to the butcher why he had a pickaxe in his hand.

"If we had lain abed till the usual time," said Solomon John, "we should have been all right."

"For here is the milkman!" said Elizabeth Eliza, as a knock was now heard at the side door.

"It is a good thing to learn," said Mr. Peterkin, "not to get up any earlier than is necessary."

Time to Think

1. Why did Mrs. Peterkin wake the family up early?

2. How important do you think it was to "secure breakfast first"?

3. What did the Peterkins hope to accomplish by creating a hole in the east wall?

4. What was the problem with opening a hole in the wall that the Peterkins did not consider?

5. What had the Peterkins not noticed because they were busy trying to make a new door?

1. What did Mr. Peterkin mean when he said, "One learns a great many things too late"?

2. At the end of the story, Mr. Peterkin said, "It is a good thing to learn not to get up any earlier than is necessary." How do you know this is not the author's moral for the story? What would make a better moral?

3. Fill in the cause and effect and problem and solution to complete each sentence.

   Cause: Because Mrs. Peterkin saw that there had been a

   _____ overnight,

   Effect: she woke the family up early in order to make

   sure they had *Brecfast* .

   ·

   Problem: Mr. Peterkin decided that it was a bad idea to

   have all of the *have   all   of   the*

   Bors on one sroe of house .

   Solution: The family decided to make a *hole*

   in the walk for a new door on the east

   side of the house.

   ·

   Problem: The back gate to the house was *Blocked*

   Buch er , so

   Solution: the *Bucher* got into the house

   through the side door.

   ·

   Cause: Because the Peterkins were busy inside the

   house, trying to create a new door,

   Effect: _____ .

   Effect: *Buche* _____ .

To focus on Plot, see page 271.

43

❖ THEME ❖

Every work of literature—whether it is a novel, short story, or poem—has a **theme**. The theme is the central idea of the work. To learn more about what a theme is, let's begin by thinking about what the theme is not.

The theme and the plot are not the same. The plot is made up of the events that the author uses to tell the story. The theme is also not the same as the moral of the story. The moral is the lesson that the author hopes the reader will learn. Not all literary works have a moral, but all of them do have a theme. Often the theme can be expressed in one word or in a short phrase. Common themes are friendship, or courage, or good overcoming evil.

The author does not usually tell the reader directly what the theme is. Instead, he suggests the theme to the reader through the words and actions of the characters. It is up to the reader to determine what the theme is. There may be more than one theme in a story or poem. Also, different readers may pick up on different themes. In contrast, the author often tells the moral of the story directly to the reader. For example, many of Aesop's fables end with a sentence that sums up the lesson to be learned from the fable.

Themes are often described as universal. That means that the theme is easily understood by people all over the world.

Think of the theme as the foundation of a house. As you look at the house, you usually do not see the foundation. You see the walls, windows, doors, and roof. You notice the materials the house was constructed from and the colors that were used. However, beneath the house is the foundation, giving it support. When you read a story

or poem, you usually
do not see the theme
right away. You notice the characters, observe the setting, and follow
the plot. Beneath all those literary elements
is the theme unifying and supporting the story.

The **theme** of family can be found in each selection in *The Peterkin Papers*. The Peterkins stick together through thick and thin and through the challenges of being snowbound. Their strong family feeling is the foundation for their stories. They may be foolish; they may see problems where none exist; they may consistently take the hardest path—but they stick together, without bickering or complaining. Each selection, however, has a different **moral**. "Don't borrow trouble" is a lesson we can learn from "The Peterkins Snowed-Up." What themes can you see in some of the other selections you have read? Remember that different readers may perceive different themes and that a selection may have more than one theme. Do any of the previous selections contain a moral? Some stories will. Understanding the theme of a selection—and possibly finding a moral—can make you think more about the author's purpose in writing the selection and add to your knowledge and enjoyment as you read.

 Time to Think

Match each **term** to the best **description**.

moral •	• central idea of the work
plot •	• lesson to learn
plot summarization •	• sequence of events
theme •	• summary of the story

THE PETERKINS TRY TO BECOME WISE

from *The Peterkin Papers* by Lucretia P. Hale

The Peterkins are back, and this time, they have
a plan for self-improvement. As usual, the family
sticks together as they put the plan into action. They
are full of inventive solutions, but will they manage to unlock the secret to becoming wise?

"If," said Mrs. Peterkin, "we could only be more wise
as a family!" How could they manage it? Agamemnon
had been to college, and the children all went to school;
but still as a family they were not wise. "It comes from
books," said one of the family. "People who have a great
many books are very wise." Then they counted up that
there were very few books in the house,—a few school-
books and Mrs. Peterkin's cook-book were all.

"That's the thing!" said Agamemnon. "We want a
library!"

"We want a library!" said Solomon John. And all of them exclaimed, "We want a library!"

"Let us think how we shall get one," said Mrs. Peterkin. "I have observed that other people think a great deal of thinking."

So they all sat and thought a great while.

Then said Agamemnon, "I will make a library. There are some boards in the wood-shed, and I have a hammer and some nails, and perhaps we can borrow some hinges, and there we have our library!"

They were all very much pleased at the idea.

"That's the book-case part," said Elizabeth Eliza; "but where are the books?"

So they sat and thought a little while, when Solomon John exclaimed, "I will make a book!"

They all looked at him in wonder.

"Yes," said Solomon John, "books will make us wise, but first I must make a book."

So they went into the parlor, and sat down to make a book. But there was no ink. What should he do for ink? Elizabeth Eliza said she had heard that nutgalls[1] and vinegar made very good ink. So they decided to make some. The little boys said they could find some nutgalls up in the woods. So they all agreed to set out and pick some. Mrs. Peterkin put on her cape-bonnet, and the little boys got into their india-rubber[2] boots, and off they went.

The nutgalls were hard to find. There was almost everything else in the woods,—chestnuts, and walnuts, and small hazel-nuts, and a great many squirrels; and they had to walk a great way before they found any nutgalls. At last they came home with a large basket and two nutgalls in it. Then came the question of the vinegar. Mrs. Peterkin had used her very last on some beets they had the day before. "Suppose we go and ask the minister's wife," said Elizabeth Eliza. So they all went to the minister's wife. She said if they wanted some good vinegar they had better set a barrel of cider down in the cellar, and in a year or two it would make very nice vinegar. But they said they wanted it that very afternoon. When the minister's wife heard this, she said she should be very glad to let them have some vinegar, and gave them a cupful to carry home.

So they stirred in the nutgalls, and by the time evening came they had very good ink.

Then Solomon John wanted a pen. Agamemnon had a steel one, but Solomon John said, "Poets always used quills."[3] Elizabeth Eliza suggested that they should go out to the poultry-yard and get a quill. But it was already dark. They had, however, two lanterns, and the little boys borrowed the neighbors'. They set out in procession for the poultry-yard. When they got there; the fowls were all at roost, so they could look at them quietly. But there were no geese! There were Guinea hens,[4] and Barbary hens,[5] and speckled hens, and Poland roosters, and bantams,[6] and ducks, and turkeys, but not one goose! "No geese but ourselves," said Mrs. Peterkin, wittily, as they returned to the house. The sight of this procession roused[7] up the village. "A torchlight procession!" cried all the boys of the town; and they gathered

---

[3] **quill**—*the hard, hollow end of a feather once used for writing*
[4] **Guinea hens** (gĭn′ē)—*female birds in the same family as pheasants*
[5] **Barbary hens** (bär′bə·rē)—*medium-sized birds known as partridges*
[6] **bantams**—*miniature birds of various breeds*
[7] **roused**—*stirred up; woke up*

round the house, shouting for the flag; and Mr. Peterkin had to invite them in, and give them cider and gingerbread, before he could explain to them that it was only his family visiting his hens.

After the crowd had dispersed,[8] Solomon John sat down to think of his writing again. Agamemnon agreed to go over to the bookstore to get a quill. They all went over with him. The bookseller was just shutting up his shop. However, he agreed to go in and get a quill, which he did, and they hurried home.

So Solomon John sat down again, but there was no paper. And now the bookstore was shut up. Mr. Peterkin suggested that the mail was about in, and perhaps he should have a letter, and then they could use the

[8] **dispersed**—*scattered*

envelope to write upon. So they all went to the post-office, and the little boys had their india-rubber boots on, and they all shouted when they found Mr. Peterkin had a letter. The post-master inquired what they were shouting about; and when they told him, he said he would give Solomon John a whole sheet of paper for his book. And they all went back rejoicing.

So Solomon John sat down, and the family all sat round the table looking at him. He had his pen, his ink, and his paper. He dipped his pen into the ink and held it over the paper, and thought a minute, and then said, "But I haven't got anything to say!"

 ## Time to Think

1. Where did the Peterkins think wisdom comes from?

2. What things did the Peterkins need in order to have a library?

3. Was it nonsense to think that Solomon John should write a book? Why or why not?

4. What could the Peterkins have done rather than trying to write their own books?

 ## I WONDER . . .

1. Which of the following best describes the moral of the story?
   a. If you own many books, you will become wise.
   b. It is good to know how to make things such as ink or paper.
   c. Wisdom starts with common sense.

2. Why is it wise to find the simplest solution to a problem rather than a complex one?

IN THE SPOTLIGHT

NARRATIVE TEXT STRUCTURE

Before an author writes the first word on paper, he has a purpose in mind. Just as builders follow blueprints or cooks use recipes, authors use text structures when writing. Text structures help authors know how to organize the information in their pieces. Authors will use different text structures depending on what they are trying to communicate. When authors wish to tell a story, they will often use a **narrative text structure**.

A narrative is either a factual or fictional story—a tale of connected events. In a narrative, the events are usually told in the order in which they happened. A narrative will have a theme, a plot, a setting, and characters; sometimes it will have a moral.

Most of the selections in this book are narratives. Look for the elements of a narrative as you read the selection "Beezus and Her Little Sister." Focus especially on the characters and the plot. Notice the events in the story line and the order in which they happen. Has the author recorded the events so that one event leads to another? Pay attention to the characters: their actions and their words. What did a character do or say that caused something to happen? How did the characters respond to events that may have been unexpected? Were any of the characters changed by the events they experienced? Focusing on the plot and the characters will make the story more enjoyable; it may also help you to discover the theme and the moral that the author hoped you would find.

 I WONDER . . .

What are the elements of a narrative?

Beezus and Her Little Sister

from *Beezus and Ramona*
by Beverly Cleary

Ramona and her big sister Beatrice (whom Ramona calls Beezus) have been favorite characters in children's literature since Beverly Cleary first introduced them in the 1950s.

In this story, Beezus has grown tired of reading to Ramona about Scoopy, the littlest steam shovel. She decides to take Ramona to the library to find a new book; but to Beezus's dismay, Ramona insists on wearing the cardboard rabbit ears she made at nursery school.

I just hope we don't meet anybody we know, Beezus thought, as they started out the front door.

But the girls had no sooner left the house when they saw Mrs. Wisser, a lady who lived in the next block, coming toward them with a friend. It was too late to turn back. Mrs. Wisser had seen them and was waving.

"Why, hello there, Beatrice," Mrs. Wisser said, when they met. "I see you have a dear little bunny with you today."

"Uh . . . yes." Beezus didn't know what else to say.

Ramona obligingly hopped up and down to make her ears flop.

Mrs. Wisser said to her friend, as if Beezus and Ramona couldn't hear, "Isn't she adorable?"

Both children knew whom Mrs. Wisser was talking about. If she had been talking about Beezus, she would have said something quite different. Such a nice girl, probably. A sweet child. Adorable, never.

"Just look at those eyes," said Mrs. Wisser.

Ramona beamed. She knew whose eyes they were talking about. Beezus knew, too, but she didn't care. Mother said blue eyes were just as pretty as brown.

Mrs. Wisser leaned over to Ramona. "What color are your eyes, sweetheart?" she asked.

"Brown and white," said Ramona promptly.

"Brown and white eyes!" exclaimed the friend. "Isn't that cunning?"

Beezus had thought it was cunning the first time she heard Ramona say it, about a year ago. Since then she had given up trying to explain to Ramona that she wasn't supposed to say she had brown and white eyes, because Ramona always answered, "My eyes *are* brown and white," and Beezus had to admit that, in a way, they were.

"And what is the little bunny's name?" asked Mrs. Wisser's friend.

"My name is Ramona Geraldine Quimby," answered Ramona, and then added generously, "My sister's name is Beezus."

"Beezus!" exclaimed the lady. "What an odd name. Is it French?"

"Oh, no," said Beezus. Wishing, as she so often did, that she had a more common nickname, like Betty or Patsy, she explained as quickly as she could how she happened to be called Beezus.

Ramona did not like to lose the attention of her audience. She hitched up the leg of her overalls and raised her knee. "See my scab?" she said proudly. "I fell down and hurt my knee and it bled and bled."

"Ramona!" Beezus was horrified. "You aren't supposed to show people your scabs."

"Why?" asked Ramona. That was one of the most exasperating[1] things about Ramona. She never seemed to understand what she was not supposed to do.

"It's a very nice scab," said Mrs. Wisser's friend, but she did not look as if she really thought it was nice.

"Well, we must be going," said Mrs. Wisser.

"Good-bye, Mrs. Wisser," said Beezus politely, and hoped that if they met anyone else they knew she could somehow manage to hide Ramona behind a bush.

"Bye-bye, Ramona," said Mrs. Wisser.

"Good-bye," said Ramona, and Beezus knew that she felt that a girl who was four years old was too grown up to say bye-bye.

Except for holding Ramona's hand crossing streets, Beezus lingered behind her the rest of the way to the library. She hoped that all the people who stopped and smiled at Ramona would not think they were together. When they reached the Glenwood Branch Library, she said, "Ramona, wouldn't you like me to carry your ears for you now?"

"No," said Ramona flatly.

Inside the library, Beezus hurried Ramona into the boys and girls' section and seated her on a little chair in front of the picture books. "See, Ramona," she whispered, "here's a book about a duck. Wouldn't you like that?"

"No," said Ramona in a loud voice.

Beezus's face turned red with embarrassment when everyone in the library looked at Ramona's ears and smiled. "Sh-h," she whispered, as Miss Greever, the

<hr>

[1] **exasperating**—*extremely annoying*

grown-ups' librarian, frowned in their direction. "You're supposed to speak quietly in the library."

Beezus selected another book. "Look, Ramona. Here's a funny story about a kitten that falls into the goldfish bowl. Wouldn't you like that?"

"No," said Ramona in a loud whisper. "I want to find my own book."

If only Miss Evans, the children's librarian, were there! She would know how to select a book for Ramona. Beezus noticed Miss Greever glance disapprovingly in their direction while the other grown-ups watched Ramona and smiled. "All right, you can look," Beezus agreed, to keep Ramona quiet. "I'll go find a book for myself."

When Beezus had selected her book, she returned to the picture-book section, where she found Ramona sitting on the bench with both arms clasped around a big flat book. "I found my book," she said, and held it up for Beezus to see. On the cover was a picture of a steam shovel with its jaws full of rocks. The title was *Big Steve the Steam Shovel.*

"Oh, Ramona," whispered Beezus in dismay. "You don't want that book."

"I do, too," insisted Ramona, forgetting to whisper. "You told me I could pick out my own book."

Under the disapproving stare of Miss Greever, Beezus gave up. Ramona was right. Beezus looked with distaste[2] at the big orange-colored book in its stout library binding. At least it would be due in two weeks, but Beezus did not feel very happy at the thought of two more weeks of steam shovels. And it just went to show how Ramona always got her own way.

---

[2] **distaste**—*a feeling of dislike*

Beezus took her book and Ramona's to Miss Greever's desk.

"Is this where you pay for the books?" asked Ramona.

"We don't have to pay for the books," said Beezus.

"Are you going to charge them?" Ramona asked.

Beezus pulled her library card out of her sweater pocket. "I show this card to the lady and she lets us keep the books for two weeks. A library isn't like a store, where you buy things."

Ramona looked as if she did not understand. "I want a card," she said.

"You have to be able to write your own name before you can have a library card," Beezus explained.

"I can write my name," said Ramona.

"Oh, Ramona," said Beezus, "you can't, either."

"Perhaps she really does know how to write her name," said Miss Greever, as she took a card out of her desk. Beezus watched doubtfully while Miss Greever asked Ramona her name and age. Then the librarian asked Ramona what her father's occupation was. When Ramona didn't understand, she asked, "What kind of work does your father do?"

"He mows the lawn," said Ramona promptly.

The librarian laughed. "I mean, how does he earn his living?"

Somehow Beezus did not like to have Miss Greever laugh at her little sister. After all, how could Ramona be expected to know what Father did? "He works for Pacific Gas and Electric Company," Beezus told the librarian.

Miss Greever wrote this down on the card and shoved it across the desk to Ramona. "Write your name on this line," she directed.

Nothing daunted,[3] Ramona grasped the pencil in her fist and began to write. She bore down so hard that the tip snapped off the lead, but she wrote on. When she laid down the pencil, Beezus picked up the card to see what she had written. The line on the card was filled with

"That's my name," said Ramona proudly.

"That's just scribbling," Beezus told her.

"It is too my name," insisted Ramona, while Miss Greever quietly dropped the card into the wastebasket. "I've watched you write and I know how."

"Here, Ramona, you can hold my card." Beezus tried to be comforting. "You can pretend it's yours."

Ramona brightened at this, and Miss Greever checked out the books on Beezus's card. As soon as they got home, Ramona demanded, "Read my new book to me."

And so Beezus began. "Big Steve was a steam shovel. He was the biggest steam shovel in the whole city. . . ." When she finished the book she had to admit she liked Big Steve better than Scoopy. His only sound effects were tooting and growling. He tooted and growled in big letters on every page. Big Steve did not shed tears or want to be a pile driver. He worked hard at being a steam shovel, and by the end of the book Beezus had learned a lot about steam shovels. Unfortunately, she

---

[3] **nothing daunted**—*with courage*

did not want to learn about steam shovels. Oh, well, she guessed she could stand two weeks of Big Steve.

"Read it again," said Ramona enthusiastically. "I like Big Steve. He's better than Scoopy."

"How would you like me to show you how to really write your name?" Beezus asked, hoping to divert[4] Ramona from steam shovels.

"O.K.," agreed Ramona.

Beezus found pencil and paper and wrote Ramona in large, careful letters across the top of the paper.

Ramona studied it critically. "I don't like it," she said at last.

"But that's the way your name is spelled," Beezus explained.

"You didn't make dots and lines," said Ramona. Seizing the pencil, she wrote,

"But, Ramona, you don't understand." Beezus took the pencil and wrote her own name on the paper. "You've seen me write Beatrice, which has an i and a t in it. See, like that. You don't have an i or a t in your name, because it isn't spelled that way."

Ramona looked skeptical. She grabbed the pencil again and wrote with a flourish,

"That's my name, because I like it," she announced. "I like to make dots and lines." Lying flat on her stomach on the floor she proceeded to fill the paper with i's and t's.

---

[4] **divert**—*to turn from a certain direction*

58

"But, Ramona, nobody's name is spelled with just . . ." Beezus stopped. What was the use? Trying to explain spelling and writing to Ramona was too complicated. Everything became difficult when Ramona was around, even an easy thing like taking a book out of the library. Well, if Ramona was happy thinking her name was spelled with *i*'s and *t*'s, she could go ahead and think it.

The next two weeks were fairly peaceful. Mother and Father soon tired of tooting and growling and, like Beezus, they looked forward to the day *Big Steve* was due at the library. Father even tried to hide the book behind the radio, but Ramona soon found it. Beezus was happy that one part of her plan had worked— Ramona had forgotten *The Littlest Steam Shovel* now that she had a better book. On Ramona's second trip to the library, perhaps Miss Evans could find a book that would make her forget steam shovels entirely.

As for Ramona, she was perfectly happy. She had three people to read aloud a book she liked, and she spent much of her time covering sheets of paper with *i*'s and *t*'s. Sometimes she wrote in pencil, sometimes she wrote in crayon, and once she wrote in ink until her mother caught her at it.

Finally, to the relief of the rest of the family, the day came when *Big Steve* had to be returned. "Come on, Ramona," said Beezus. "It's time to go to the library for another book."

"I have a book," said Ramona, who was lying on her stomach writing her version of her name on a piece of paper with purple crayon.

"No, it belongs to the library," Beezus explained, glad that for once Ramona couldn't possibly get her own way.

"It's my book," said Ramona, crossing several t's with a flourish.

"Beezus is right, dear," observed Mother. "Run along and get *Big Steve*."

Ramona looked sulky, but she went into the bedroom. In a few minutes she appeared with *Big Steve* in her hand and a satisfied expression on her face. "It's my book," she announced. "I wrote my name in it."

Mother looked alarmed. "What do you mean, Ramona? Let me see." She took the book and opened it. Every page in the book was covered with enormous purple *i*'s and *t*'s in Ramona's very best handwriting.

"Mother!" cried Beezus. "Look what she's done! And in crayon so it won't erase."

"Ramona Quimby," said Mother. "You're a very naughty girl! Why did you do a thing like that?"

"It's my book," said Ramona stubbornly. "I like it."

"Mother, what am I going to do?" Beezus demanded. "It's checked out on my card and I'm responsible. They won't let me take any more books out of the library, and I won't have anything to read, and it will all be Ramona's fault. She's always spoiling my fun and it isn't fair!" Beezus didn't know what she would do without her library card. She couldn't get along without library books. She just couldn't, that was all.

"I do *not* spoil your fun," stormed Ramona.

60

"You have all the fun. I can't read and it isn't fair."
Ramona's words ended in a howl as she buried her face
in her mother's skirt.

"I couldn't read when I was your age and I didn't
have someone to read to me all the time, so it is too
fair," argued Beezus. "You always get your own way,
because you're the youngest."

"I do not!" shouted Ramona. "And you don't read
all the time. You're mean!"

"I am *not* mean," Beezus shouted back.

"Children!" cried Mother. "Stop it, both of you!
Ramona, you were a very naughty girl!" A loud sniff
came from Ramona. "And, Beezus," her mother continued, "the library won't take your card away from
you. If you'll get my purse I'll give you some money to
pay for the damage to the book. Take Ramona along
with you, explain what happened, and the librarian will
tell you how much to pay."

This made Beezus feel better. Ramona sulked all
the way to the library, but when they got there Beezus
was pleased to see that Miss Evans, the children's
librarian, was sitting behind the desk. Miss Evans was
the kind of librarian who would understand about little
sisters.

"Hello, Beatrice," said Miss Evans. "Is this your
little sister I've heard so much about?"

Beezus wondered what Miss Evans had heard about
Ramona. "Yes, this is Ramona," she said and went on
hesitantly, "and, Miss Evans, she—"

"I'm a bad girl," interrupted Ramona, smiling win-
ningly at the librarian.

"Oh, you are?" said Miss Evans. "What did you do?"

"I wrote in a book," said Ramona, not the least ashamed. "I wrote in purple crayon and it will never, ever erase. Never, never, never."

Embarrassed, Beezus handed Miss Evans *Big Steve the Steam Shovel*. "Mother gave me the money to pay for the damage," she explained.

The librarian turned the pages of the book. "Well, you didn't miss a page, did you?" she finally said to Ramona.

"No," said Ramona, pleased with herself. "And it will never, never—"

"I'm awfully sorry," interrupted Beezus. "After this I'll try to keep our library books where she can't reach them."

Miss Evans consulted[5] a file of little cards in a drawer. "Since every page in the book was damaged and the library can no longer use it, I'll have to ask you to pay for the whole book. I'm sorry, but this is the rule. It will cost two dollars and fifty cents."

Two dollars and fifty cents! What a lot of things that would have bought, Beezus reflected, as she pulled three folded dollar bills out of her pocket and handed them to the librarian. Miss Evans put the money in a drawer and gave Beezus fifty cents in change.

Then Miss Evans took a rubber stamp and stamped something inside the book. By twisting her head around, Beezus could see that the word was *Discarded*. "There!" Miss Evans said, pushing the book across the desk. "You have paid for it, so now it's yours."

Beezus stared at the librarian. "You mean . . . to keep?"

"That's right," answered Miss Evans.

Ramona grabbed the book. "It's mine. I told you it was mine!" Then she turned to Beezus and said

---

[5] **consulted**—*looked for information*

triumphantly, "You said people didn't buy books at the library and now you just bought one!"

"Buying a book and paying for damage are not the same thing," Miss Evans pointed out to Ramona.

Beezus could see that Ramona didn't care. The book was hers, wasn't it? It was paid for and she could keep it. And that's not fair, thought Beezus. Ramona shouldn't get her own way when she had been naughty.

"But, Miss Evans," protested Beezus, "if she spoils a book she shouldn't get to keep it. Now every time she finds a book she likes she will . . ." Beezus did not go on. She knew very well what Ramona would do, but she wasn't going to say it out loud in front of her.

"I see what you mean." Miss Evans looked thoughtful. "Give me the book, Ramona," she said.

Doubtfully Ramona handed her the book.

"Ramona, do you have a library card?" Miss Evans asked.

Ramona shook her head.

"Then Beezus must have taken the book out on her card," said Miss Evans. "So the book belongs to Beezus."

Why, of course! Why hadn't she thought of that before? It was her book, not Ramona's. "Oh, thank you," said Beezus gratefully, as Miss Evans handed the book to her. She could do anything she wanted with it.

For once Ramona didn't know what to say. She scowled and looked as if she were building up to a tantrum. "You've got to read it to me," she said at last.

"Not unless I feel like it," said Beezus. "After all, it's my book," she couldn't resist adding.

"That's no fair!" Ramona looked as if she were about to howl.

"It is too fair," said Beezus calmly. "And if you have a tantrum I won't read to you at all."

Suddenly, as if she had decided Beezus meant what she said, Ramona stopped scowling. "O.K.," she said cheerfully.

Beezus watched her carefully for a minute. Yes, she really was being agreeable, thought Beezus with a great feeling of relief. And now that she did not have to read *Big Steve* unless she wanted to, Beezus felt she would not mind reading it once in a while. "Come on, Ramona," she said. "Maybe I'll have time to read to you before Father comes home."

"O.K.," said Ramona happily, as she took Beezus's hand.

Miss Evans smiled at the girls as they started to leave. "Good luck, Beatrice," she said.

As the girls leave the library, Beezus is relieved that all has ended well. But has it really? Ramona is still Ramona, bursting with energy and full of creativity—but not always in a good way. What will she do next? Whether it involves all of the apples that Mother has stored away for the future, or the birthday cake for Beezus that is baking in the oven, Ramona is certain to create mischief. Beezus begins to wonder if she and Ramona will ever have a close sisterly relationship like the one that exists between Mother and her sister. For the rest of the tale of these two very different sisters, you will want to read *Beezus and Ramona*.

Time to Think

1. What did Ramona do that embarrassed Beezus?

2. Why did Ramona think that the library book was hers?

3. Why didn't Beezus want the librarian to give Ramona the book after it was paid for?

I WONDER . . .

1. Although Beezus is embarrassed by the way Ramona behaved in the library, the adults in the library smiled at Ramona's behavior. Why do you think this is?

2. Ramona and Beezus had an argument over who has all the fun. What does that tell you about the perspective of each of the sisters?

3. Do you think the librarian's solution to the problem of the damaged book was a wise solution? Why or why not?

THINK ON THESE THINGS

Although the theme of family is found throughout *Beezus and Ramona,* another strong theme is understanding. At the beginning of the story, the sisters do not understand each other. Beezus thinks that Ramona gets whatever she wants, and Ramona thinks that Beezus has all the fun because she can do more things. By the end of the excerpt, the two begin to understand each other. Beezus begins to see things from Ramona's perspective, and Ramona begins to understand that Beezus means business.

Philippians 2:4 says, "Look not every man on his own things, but every man also on the things of others."

How can understanding this principle help you show patience with others? Do you relate more to Beezus or Ramona?

To focus on Narrative Text Structure, see page 272.

IN THE SPOTLIGHT

❧ CHARACTER DEVELOPMENT ❧

Think back to all the books and stories you have read recently. Who was your favorite character? What made the character appealing? Was the character so fantastical that he could exist only in the world of imagination? Or was she so true-to-life that you could easily believe that you might find her living next door? A good author works to develop strong characters that captivate the reader. Characters may be realistic or absurd, but the author can make them believable when he builds characters whose personalities, motives, and actions suit the world the author has created. The story line the author chooses and the characters he creates are closely related. After all, it is the character who lives within the story, shapes the events of the plot, and can be shaped by them.

Characters can be classified by the way they react to the events in their story line. Some characters grow as the story progresses. Often it is the **main character** whose transformation is at the heart of the story. Other characters remain mostly unchanged throughout the story. Such characters are usually **secondary characters**, created by the author to support the main character. In the selection "Beezus and Her Little Sister," Ramona is one of the main characters, yet she remains mostly unchanged as the story line progresses. However, we see her sister Beezus—the other main character—grow in understanding. Beezus begins to realize how

Ramona thinks and why she acts as she does. That realization changes Beezus's reaction to some of Ramona's quirky behaviors.

Another way to classify a character is by how **true-to-life**, or **multidimensional**, his or her personality is. Beezus and Ramona are both very lifelike—they seem like they could be children you know. They could step right out from the pages of the book and into your neighborhood or your school. On the other hand, some characters have just one or two principal personality traits. That kind of character is **one-dimensional**; often you could describe them in one word. The author has created them to represent a particular characteristic or to move the story's plot forward. In *The Peterkin Papers*, the Peterkins are one-dimensional characters. We know only one thing about them: they have no common sense. The author uses this single characteristic humorously to illustrate that knowledge is not the same as wisdom.

Fictional characters can be classified into more than one category. Beezus is a well-developed character who changes throughout the story. Ramona is equally well-rounded, but she remains essentially unchanged. The Peterkins are less true-to-life, but their one characteristic—lack of common sense—is what drives the action of the story. They remain the same throughout the selection, without any sign that they will ever change.

Fictional characters may be lifelike or one-dimensional. They may remain unchanged throughout the story, or they may develop and grow as the story progresses. Ultimately, the author's skill and imagination in creating a variety of characters help make a book memorable and enjoyable.

 I WONDER . . .

Choose from the following answers.

a. one-dimensional
b. secondary
c. true-to-life

1. The role of this character is to support the main character.

2. These characters can often be described in one word.

3. These characters are like people you know.

The Way to Do It

Mary Mapes Dodge

Characters are developed not only in books but also on stage. If an actor only reads or recites his lines, his character may feel one-dimensional. But when an actor uses expressive actions and shows emotion, he brings his character to life. "The Way to Do It" explains how an actor can portray a multidimensional character.

I'll tell you how I speak a piece:
First, I make my bow;
Then I bring my words out clear
And plain as I know how.

Next, I throw my hands up *so!*
Then I lift my eyes—
That's to let my hearers know
Something doth surprise.

69

Next, I grin and show my teeth,
    Nearly every one;
Shake my shoulders, hold my sides:
    That's the sign of fun.

Next, I start and knit my brow,
    Hold my head erect:
Something's wrong, you see, and I
    Decidedly object.

Now I start, and with a leap
    Seize an airy dagger.
"WRETCH!" I cry. That's tragedy,
    Every soul to stagger.

Then I let my voice grow faint,
    Gasp and hold my breath;
Tumble down and plunge about:
    That's a villain's death.

Quickly then I come to life,
    Perfectly restored;
With a bow my speech is done.
    Now you'll please applaud.

I WONDER . . .

1. What good advice is given in the first stanza?

2. How does the narrator of this poem express emotion when reciting a piece?

3. How could you use the advice given in this poem to improve your own oral reading?

IN THE SPOTLIGHT

❧ AUTHOR'S PURPOSE ❧

Before an author picks up his pen, he has a **purpose** for writing. His purpose will determine the words and text structure he uses. The reader can usually determine the purpose by reading carefully.

Sometimes an author writes to inform the reader about a particular topic; but often, an author writes for the purpose of simply entertaining the reader. In this case, the author wants to tell you a story that you will enjoy. Much fiction—whether a narrative, a poem, or even a book full of jokes—is written to entertain. An author will use intriguing characters, action-packed scenes, and humorous stories to entertain.

At times, an author writes for the purpose of teaching a lesson. The author wants to write a story that communicates an important truth. Any piece of literature—whether fiction, nonfiction, or poetry—can teach a lesson. Sometimes, the lesson is directly stated in the piece. At other times, the author wants readers to draw the lesson from the story's characters and events.

An author may have more than one purpose in mind as he sets out to write. Many entertaining stories also teach valuable lessons that readers can apply to their lives. Understanding the author's purpose can give you a fuller appreciation for what you are reading.

I WONDER . . .

Choose from the following answers.

a. entertain   **b.** inform   **c.** teach

1. An author includes amusing stories to _____ the reader.

2. An author communicates truth to _____ a lesson.

3. An author writes about a topic to _____ the reader.

MEET THE AUTHOR
Eleanor Estes

From a young age, Eleanor Estes (1906–1988) loved stories. Her father died when she was young, and her mother supported the family as a dressmaker. Both of Eleanor's parents loved books, and her mother was a very gifted storyteller. After graduating from high school in 1923, Eleanor began working at the New Haven Free Library as a children's librarian. In 1931, she received a scholarship to the Pratt Institute, where she studied library science. She also met Rice Estes, a fellow librarian, while she was a student there; the couple married in 1932. Estes went on to work as a children's librarian in various branches of the New York City Public Library. Her husband eventually became a professor of library science.

In 1941, Estes became seriously ill with tuberculosis and spent a year confined to her bed. During this time, she began writing her first book, *The Moffats*, which she based on her own childhood.

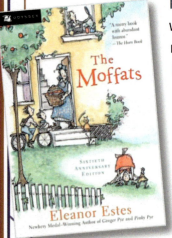

The Moffat family, four children and their widowed mother, live in Cranbury, Connecticut, a fictional town based on Eleanor's hometown of West Haven, Connecticut. Mrs. Moffat, like Eleanor's mother, supports her family as a seamstress. Estes modeled the character of Janey Moffat on herself; Rufus Moffat was based on her younger brother Teddy. *The Moffats* was well received, and Estes quickly followed it with two more books about the family,

The Middle Moffat and Rufus M., both of which were Newbery Honor books.

Eleanor Estes's next book, *The Hundred Dresses*, published in 1944, was another Newbery Honor book. Like her previous books, it is based on Estes's own experiences as a child. Unlike her books about the Moffat family, *The Hundred Dresses* centers on an act of unkindness and its consequences.

During her writing career, Eleanor Estes authored nineteen children's books. Among them was *Ginger Pye*, which, in 1952, won the Newbery Medal, the highest honor awarded in children's literature. Forty years after publishing *The Moffats*, Estes wrote the fourth and final book in the series, *The Moffat Museum*. Many years after her death, Eleanor Estes remains one of the mid-twentieth century's most highly regarded children's authors.

 ## Time to Think

1. Where did Eleanor Estes grow up, and why is this important to her books about the Moffats?

2. Where did Eleanor work after graduating from high school?

3. What event led to the writing of Estes's first book, *The Moffats*?

4. Which of Eleanor Estes's books earned Newbery Honors?

5. How was *The Hundred Dresses* similar to Estes's previous books about the Moffats? How was it different?

I WONDER . . .

What is the purpose for this selection?
   a. to entertain
   b. to inform
   c. to teach a lesson

an excerpt from

THE HUNDRED DRESSES

Eleanor Estes

Every morning, Maddie and her best friend Peggy wait for Wanda Petronski to come up the road to school so that they can play the "dresses game." All the girls in school enjoy the game—at least, all the girls except Wanda. On this particular morning, however, Wanda does not come down the road. Peggy and Maddie are actually late to school, arriving after class has begun. As Maddie settles in, she wonders what happened to Wanda.

The Dresses Game

After Peggy and Maddie stopped feeling like intruders in a class that had already begun, they looked across the room and noticed that Wanda was not in her seat. Furthermore her desk was dusty and looked as though she hadn't been there yesterday either. Come to think of it, they hadn't seen her yesterday. They had waited for her a little while but had forgotten about her when they reached school.

They often waited for Wanda Petronski—to have fun with her.

Wanda lived way up on Boggins Heights, and Boggins Heights was no place to live. It was a good place to go and pick wildflowers in the summer, but you always held your breath till you got safely past old man Svenson's yellow house. People in the town said old man Svenson was no good. He didn't work and, worse still, his house and yard were disgracefully dirty, with rusty tin cans strewn about and even an old straw hat. He lived alone with his dog and his cat. No wonder, said the people of the town. Who would live with him? And many stories circulated about him and the stories were the kind that made people scurry past his house even in broad daylight and hope not to meet him.

Beyond Svenson's there were a few small scattered frame houses, and in one of these Wanda Petronski lived with her father and her brother Jake.

Wanda Petronski. Most of the children in Room 13 didn't have names like that. They had names easy to say, like Thomas, Smith, or Allen. There was one boy named Bounce, Willie Bounce, and people thought that was funny but not funny in the same way that Petronski was.

Wanda didn't have any friends. She came to school alone and went home alone. She always wore a faded blue dress that didn't hang right. It was clean, but it looked as though it had never been ironed properly. She didn't have any friends, but a lot of girls talked to her. They waited for her under the maple trees on the corner of Oliver Street. Or they surrounded her in the school yard as she stood watching some little girls play hop-scotch on the worn hard ground.

"Wanda," Peggy would say in a most courteous manner, as though she were talking to Miss Mason or to the principal perhaps. "Wanda," she'd say, giving one of her friends a nudge, "tell us. How many dresses did you say you had hanging up in your closet?"

"A hundred," said Wanda.

"A hundred!" exclaimed all the girls incredulously, and the little girls would stop playing hopscotch and listen.

"Yeah, a hundred, all lined up," said Wanda. Then her thin lips drew together in silence.

"What are they like? All silk, I bet," said Peggy.

"Yeah, all silk, all colors."

"Velvet, too?"

"Yeah, velvet, too. A hundred dresses," repeated Wanda stolidly.[1] "All lined up in my closet."

Then they'd let her go. And then before she'd gone very far, they couldn't help bursting into shrieks and peals of laughter.

A hundred dresses! Obviously the only dress Wanda had was the blue one she wore every day. So what did she say she had a hundred for? What a story! And the girls laughed derisively, while Wanda moved over to the sunny place by the ivy-covered brick wall of the school

---

[1] **stolidly**—*showing little or no emotion*

building where she usually stood and waited for the bell to ring.

But if the girls had met her at the corner of Oliver Street, they'd carry her along with them for a way, stopping every few feet for more incredulous questions. And it wasn't always dresses they talked about. Sometimes it was hats, or coats, or even shoes.

"How many shoes did you say you had?"

"Sixty."

"Sixty! Sixty pairs or sixty shoes?"

"Sixty pairs. All lined up in my closet."

"Yesterday you said fifty."

"Now I got sixty."

Cries of exaggerated politeness greeted this.

"All alike?" said the girls.

"Oh, no. Every pair is different. All colors. All lined up." And Wanda would shift her eyes quickly from Peggy to a distant spot, as though she were looking far ahead, looking but not seeing anything.

Then the outer fringe of the crowd of girls would break away gradually, laughing, and little by little, in pairs, the group would disperse. Peggy, who had thought up this game, and Maddie, her inseparable friend, were always the last to leave. And finally Wanda would move up the street, her eyes dull and her mouth closed tight, hitching her left shoulder every now and then in the funny way she had, finishing the walk to school alone.

Peggy was not really cruel. She protected small children from bullies. And she cried for hours if she saw an animal mistreated. If anybody had said to her, "Don't you think that is a cruel way to treat Wanda?" she would have been very surprised. Cruel? What did the girl want to go and say she had a hundred dresses for? Anybody could tell that was a lie. Why did she want to lie? And she wasn't just an ordinary person, else why would she have a name like that? Anyway, they never made her cry.

As for Maddie, this business of asking Wanda every day how many dresses and how many hats and how many this and that she had was bothering her. Maddie was poor herself. She usually wore somebody's hand-me-down clothes. Thank goodness she didn't live up on Boggins Heights or have a funny name. And her forehead didn't shine the way Wanda's round one did. What did she use on it? Sapolio?[2] That's what all the girls wanted to know.

Sometimes when Peggy was asking Wanda those questions in that mock polite voice, Maddie felt embarrassed and studied the marbles in the palm of her hand, rolling them around and saying nothing herself. Not that she felt sorry for Wanda exactly. She would never have paid any attention to Wanda if Peggy hadn't invented the dresses game. But suppose Peggy and all the others started in on her next! She wasn't as poor as Wanda perhaps, but she was poor. Of course she would have more sense than to say a hundred dresses. Still she would not like them to begin on her. Not at all! Oh, dear! She did wish Peggy would stop teasing Wanda Petronski.

---

[2] **Sapolio**— *a soap brand used in the late 1800s and early 1900s*

A Bright Blue Day

Somehow Maddie could not buckle down to work.

She sharpened her pencil, turning it around carefully in the little red sharpener, letting the shavings fall in a neat heap on a piece of scrap paper, and trying not to get any of the dust from the lead on her clean arithmetic paper.

A slight frown puckered her forehead. In the first place she didn't like being late to school. And in the second place she kept thinking about Wanda. Somehow Wanda's desk, though empty, seemed to be the only thing she saw when she looked over to that side of the room.

How had the hundred dresses game begun in the first place? she asked herself impatiently. It was hard to remember the time when they hadn't played that game with Wanda; hard to think all the way back from now, when the hundred dresses was like the daily dozen, to then, when everything seemed much nicer. Oh, yes. She remembered. It had begun that day when Cecile first wore her new red dress. Suddenly the whole scene flashed swiftly and vividly before Maddie's eyes.

It was a bright blue day in September. No, it must have been October, because when she and Peggy were coming to school, arms around each other and singing, Peggy had said, "You know what? This must be the kind of day they mean when they say, 'October's bright blue weather.'"

Maddie remembered that because afterwards it didn't seem like bright blue weather anymore, although the weather had not changed in the slightest.

As they turned from shady Oliver Street into Maple, they both blinked. For now the morning sun shone straight in their eyes. Besides that, bright flashes of color came from a group of a half dozen or more girls across the street. Their sweaters and jackets and dresses, blues and golds and reds, and one crimson one in particular, caught the sun's rays like bright pieces of glass.

A crisp, fresh wind was blowing, swishing their skirts and blowing their hair in their eyes. The girls were all exclaiming and shouting and each one was trying to talk louder than the others. Maddie and Peggy joined the group, and the laughing, and the talking.

"Hi, Peg! Hi, Maddie!" they were greeted warmly. "Look at Cecile!"

What they were all exclaiming about was the dress that Cecile had on—a crimson dress with cap and socks to match. It was a bright new dress and very pretty. Everyone was admiring it and admiring Cecile. For long, slender Cecile wore fancier clothes than most of them. And she had her black satin bag slung over her shoulders.

Maddie sat down on the granite curbstone to tie her shoelaces. She listened happily to what they were saying. They all seemed especially jolly today, probably because it was such a bright day. Everything sparkled. Way down

at the end of the street the sun shimmered and turned
to silver the blue water of the bay. Maddie picked up a
piece of broken mirror and flashed a small circle of light
edged with rainbow colors onto the houses, the trees,
and the top of the telegraph pole.

And it was then that Wanda had come along with her
brother Jake.

They didn't often come to school together. Jake
had to get to school very early because he helped old
Mr. Heany, the school janitor, with the furnace, or
raking up the dry leaves, or other odd jobs before school
opened. Today he must be late.

Even Wanda looked pretty in this sunshine, and her
pale blue dress looked like a piece of the sky in summer;
and that old gray toboggan cap she wore—it must

be something Jake had found—looked almost jaunty.[3] Maddie watched them absentmindedly as she flashed her piece of broken mirror here and there. And only absentmindedly she noticed Wanda stop short when they reached the crowd of laughing and shouting girls.

"Come on," Maddie heard Jake say. "I gotta hurry. I gotta get the doors opened and ring the bell."

"You go the rest of the way," said Wanda. "I want to stay here."

Jake shrugged and went on up Maple Street. Wanda slowly approached the group of girls. With each step forward, before she put her foot down she seemed to hesitate for a long, long time. She approached the group as a timid animal might, ready to run if anything alarmed it.

Even so, Wanda's mouth was twisted into the vaguest[4] suggestion of a smile. She must feel happy, too, because everybody must feel happy on such a day.

As Wanda joined the outside fringe of girls, Maddie stood up, too, and went over close to Peggy to get a good look at Cecile's new dress herself. She forgot about Wanda, and more girls kept coming up, enlarging the group and all exclaiming about Cecile's new dress.

"Isn't it lovely!" said one.

"Yeah, I have a blue dress, but it's not as pretty as that," said another.

"My mother just bought me a plaid, one of the Stuart plaids."

"I got a new dress for school."

"I'm gonna make my mother get me one just like Cecile's."

---

[3] jaunty—*stylish*
[4] vaguest—*most unclear*

Everyone was talking to everybody else. Nobody said anything to Wanda, but there she was, a part of the crowd. The girls closed in a tighter circle around Cecile, still talking all at once and admiring her, and Wanda was somehow enveloped in the group. Nobody talked to Wanda, but nobody even thought about her being there.

Maybe, thought Maddie, remembering what had happened next, maybe she figured all she'd have to do was say something and she'd really be one of the girls. And this would be an easy thing to do because all they were doing was talking about dresses.

Maddie was standing next to Peggy. Wanda was standing next to Peggy on the other side. All of a sudden, Wanda impulsively touched Peggy's arm and said something. Her light blue eyes were shining and she looked excited like the rest of the girls.

"What?" asked Peggy. For Wanda had spoken very softly.

Wanda hesitated a moment and then she repeated her words firmly.

"I got a hundred dresses home."

"That's what I thought you said. A hundred dresses. A hundred!" Peggy's voice raised itself higher and higher.

"Hey, kids!" she yelled. "This girl's got a hundred dresses."

Silence greeted this, and the crowd which had centered around Cecile and her new finery now centered curiously around Wanda and Peggy. The girls eyed Wanda, first incredulously, then suspiciously.

"A hundred dresses?" they said. "Nobody could have a hundred dresses."

"I have though."

"Wanda has a hundred dresses."

"Where are they then?"

"In my closet."

"Oh, you don't wear them to school."

"No. For parties."

"Oh, you mean you don't have any everyday dresses."

"Yes, I have all kinds of dresses."

"Why don't you wear them to school?"

For a moment Wanda was silent to this. Her lips drew together. Then she repeated stolidly as though it were a lesson learned in school, "A hundred of them. All lined up in my closet."

"Oh, I see," said Peggy, talking like a grown-up person. "The child has a hundred dresses, but she wouldn't wear them to school. Perhaps she's worried of getting ink or chalk on them."

With this everybody fell to laughing and talking at once. Wanda looked stolidly at them, pursing[5] her lips together, wrinkling her forehead up so that the gray toboggan slipped way down on her brow. Suddenly from down the street the school gong[6] rang its first warning.

"Oh, come on, hurry," said Maddie, relieved. "We'll be late."

"Good-bye, Wanda," said Peggy. "Your hundred dresses sound bee-you-tiful."

More shouts of laughter greeted this, and off the girls ran, laughing and talking and forgetting Wanda and her hundred dresses. Forgetting until tomorrow and the next day and the next, when Peggy, seeing her coming to school, would remember and ask her about the hundred

---

[5] **pursing**—*pressing into a thin line*

[6] **gong**—*a saucer-shaped bell that produces a loud ring when struck by a hammer*

84

dresses. For now Peggy seemed to think a day was lost if she had not had some fun with Wanda, winning the approving laughter of the girls.

Yes, that was the way it had all begun, the game of the hundred dresses. It all happened so suddenly and unexpectedly, with everybody falling right in, that even if you felt uncomfortable as Maddie had there wasn't anything you could do about it. Maddie wagged her head up and down. Yes, she repeated to herself, that was the way it began, that day, that bright blue day.

And she wrapped up her shavings and went to the front of the room to empty them in the teacher's basket.

The Contest

Now today, even though she and Peggy had been late to school, Maddie was glad she had not had to make fun of Wanda. She worked her arithmetic problems absentmind-edly. Eight times eight . . . let's see . . . nothing she could do about making fun of Wanda. She wished she had the nerve to write Peggy a note, because she knew she'd never have the courage to speak right out to Peggy, to say, "Hey, Peg, let's stop asking Wanda how many dresses she has."

When she finished her arithmetic, she did start a note to Peggy. Suddenly she paused and shuddered. She pictured herself in the school yard, a new target for Peggy and the girls. Peggy might ask her where she got the dress she had on, and Maddie would have to say that it was one of Peggy's old ones that Maddie's mother had tried to disguise with new trimmings so that no one in Room 13 would recognize it.

If only Peggy would decide of her own accord to stop having fun with Wanda. Oh, well! Maddie ran her hand through her short blond hair as though to push the uncomfortable thoughts away. What difference did it make? Slowly Maddie tore the note she had started into bits. She was Peggy's best friend, and Peggy was the best-liked girl in the whole room. Peggy could not possibly do anything that was really wrong, she thought.

As for Wanda, she was just some girl who lived up on Boggins Heights and stood alone in the school yard. Nobody in the room thought about Wanda at all except when it was her turn to stand up for oral reading. Then they all hoped she would hurry up and finish and sit down, because it took her forever to read a paragraph. Sometimes she stood up and just looked at her book and couldn't, or wouldn't, read at all. The teacher tried to help her, but she'd just stand there until the teacher told her to sit down. Maybe she was just timid. The only time she talked was in the school yard about her hundred dresses. Maddie remembered her telling about one of her

dresses, a pale blue one with cerise[7]-colored trimmings. And she remembered another that was brilliant jungle green with a red sash. "You'd look like a Christmas tree in that," the girls had said in pretended admiration.

Thinking about Wanda and her hundred dresses all lined up in the closet, Maddie began to wonder who was going to win the drawing and color contest. For girls, this contest consisted of designing dresses, and for boys, of designing motorboats. Probably Peggy would win the girls' medal. Peggy drew better than anyone else in the room. At least that's what everybody thought. Oh, Maddie did hope Peggy would win. Hope so? She was sure Peggy would win. Well, tomorrow the teacher was going to announce the winners. Then they'd know.

Thoughts of Wanda sank further and further from Maddie's mind, and by the time the history lesson began she had forgotten all about her.

The Hundred Dresses

The next day it was drizzling. Maddie and Peggy hurried to school under Peggy's umbrella. Naturally on a day like this they didn't wait for Wanda Petronski on the corner of Oliver Street, the street that far, far away, under the railroad tracks and up the hill, led to Boggins Heights. Anyway they weren't taking chances on being late today, because today was important.

"Do you think Miss Mason will surely announce the winners today?" asked Peggy.

"Oh, I hope so, the minute we get in," said Maddie, and added, "Of course you'll win, Peg."

"Hope so," said Peggy eagerly.

---

[7] **cerise**—*deep, dark red; from the French word for cherry*

The minute they entered the classroom they stopped short and gasped. There were drawings all over the room, on every ledge and windowsill, tacked to the tops of the blackboards, spread over the bird charts, dazzling colors and brilliant lavish[8] designs, all drawn on great sheets of wrapping paper.

There must have been a hundred of them all lined up!

8 **lavish**—*extravagant; excessive in amount*

These must be the drawings for the contest. They were! Everybody stopped and whistled or murmured admiringly.

As soon as the class had assembled Miss Mason announced the winners. Jack Beggles had won for the boys, she said, and his design of an outboard motorboat was on exhibition in Room 12, along with the sketches by all the other boys.

"As for the girls," she said, "although just one or two sketches were submitted by most, one girl—and Room 13 should be very proud of her—this one girl actually drew one hundred designs—all different and all beautiful. In the opinion of the judges, any one of her drawings is worthy of winning the prize. I am happy to say that Wanda Petronski is the winner of the girls' medal. Unfortunately Wanda has been absent from school for some days and is not here to receive the applause that is due her. Let us hope she will be back tomorrow. Now, class, you may file around the room quietly and look at her exquisite drawings."

The children burst into applause, and even the boys were glad to have a chance to stamp on the floor, put their fingers in their mouths and whistle, though they were not interested in dresses. Maddie and Peggy were among the first to reach the blackboard to look at the drawings.

"Look, Peg," whispered Maddie, "there's that blue one she told us about. Isn't it beautiful?"

"Yeah," said Peggy, "and here's that green one. Boy, and I thought I could draw!"

While the class was circling the room, the monitor from the principal's office brought Miss Mason a note. Miss Mason read it several times and studied it thought-fully for a while. Then she clapped her hands and said, "Attention, class. Everyone back to his seat."

When the shuffling of feet had stopped and the room was still and quiet, Miss Mason said, "I have a letter from Wanda's father that I want to read to you."

Miss Mason stood there a moment and the silence in the room grew tense and expectant.[9] The teacher adjusted

---

[9] **expectant**—*full of expectation; to expect something*

her glasses slowly and deliberately. Her manner indicated that what was coming—this letter from Wanda's father— was a matter of great importance. Everybody listened closely as Miss Mason read the brief note:

Dear teacher: My Wanda will not come to your school anymore. Jake also. Now we move away to big city. No more calling names. No more ask why funny name. Plenty of funny names in the big city.

Yours truly, Jan Petronski

Eventually, Maddie and Peggy realized that the hundred dresses did exist. They were "all lined up" in Wanda's imagination, and she brought them to life with her artistic talent. But now that she has moved away, will she ever find out that she is the winner of the contest? More importantly, will Maddie and Peggy ever have the opportunity to make things right with her? The answers to these questions and more are found in the conclusion of *The Hundred Dresses*.

Time to Think

1. What was the "dresses game"?

2. Why did the girls play this game?

3. Why do you think Wanda made up her story about the hundred dresses?

4. Why was Maddie bothered by the way Peggy treated Wanda?

I WONDER . . .

1. Which of the following statements best expresses the author's purpose?
   a. to describe what it is like to be an outsider
   b. to encourage readers to develop their talents, as Wanda developed her talent for art
   c. to tell a realistic story about treating others as you would like to be treated

2. What change do you begin to see in Peggy at the conclusion?

3. How do you think the story ends? Predict an ending.

THINK ON THESE THINGS

Perhaps the story didn't end as you expected. While "kindness" could be the theme, it is actually missing from the story. Peggy acted unkindly toward Wanda. She did not harm Wanda physically. She did not threaten her. However, she was a bully because she repeatedly singled Wanda out with cruel remarks. Peggy's behavior was bad in itself, but even worse, she encouraged the other girls in her class to treat Wanda unkindly. Maddie never said anything to Wanda, but her silence was another form of unkindness. She saw wrong being done, yet she said nothing. Maddie's silence told Wanda that Maddie agreed with the unkind behavior of the others.

2 Peter 1:3–7 tells us that God's promises have been given to us to help us to be more like Jesus. Listed among the character qualities we should demonstrate is brotherly kindness. How can you show kindness to those around you? What could you do to encourage kind behavior in your group of friends?

To focus on Character Development, see page 273.

Try, Try Again

T. H. Palmer

'Tis a lesson you should heed,
    Try, try again;
If at first you don't succeed,
    Try, try again;
Then your courage should appear,
For, if you will persevere,
You will conquer, never fear;
    Try, try again.

Once or twice though you should fail,
    Try, try again;
If you would at last prevail,
    Try, try again;
If we strive, 'tis no disgrace
Though we do not win the race;
What should you do in the case?
    Try, try again.

IN THE SPOTLIGHT

REPETITION

Sometimes lines, phrases, and even stanzas are repeated in poetry. This technique, which is called **repetition**, is used by writers to achieve several goals. Repetition can help create the rhythm of the poem; it can also emphasize an emotion. Because repetition makes an idea more memorable, a good writer thinks carefully about which line or phrase he wants to repeat. The repeated line often highlights the theme of the poem. When you see repetition in a poem, notice that the author is pointing out something important.

I WONDER . . .

1. In the poem "Try, Try Again," how many times does the line "Try, try again" appear?

2. Notice that the rhythm of the repeated line is different from the rhythm of any of the other lines in the poem. What feeling does the repetition of that particular rhythm help to create?
   a. courage   b. fear   c. joy   d. surprise

3. Which of the following themes best describes "Try, Try Again"?
   a. courage
   b. family
   c. persistence

4. Summarize the poem in your own words.

_____

_____

_____

_____

_____

_____

_____

Chloe and the C3

Bethany Urbina

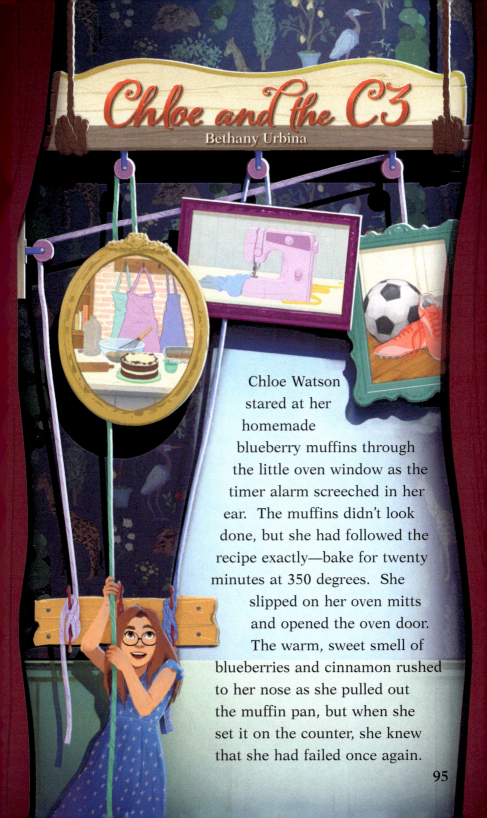

Chloe Watson stared at her homemade blueberry muffins through the little oven window as the timer alarm screeched in her ear. The muffins didn't look done, but she had followed the recipe exactly—bake for twenty minutes at 350 degrees. She slipped on her oven mitts and opened the oven door. The warm, sweet smell of blueberries and cinnamon rushed to her nose as she pulled out the muffin pan, but when she set it on the counter, she knew that she had failed once again.

95

The muffin tops were still jiggly, and all the blueberries had sunk to the bottom of the muffins.

"What am I doing wrong?" Chloe asked herself out loud.

"Do I smell blueberry muffins?" her dad asked as he rounded the corner into the kitchen. Chloe forced herself to smile at him as she took off her oven mitts and her apron.

"Don't get too excited, Dad," she told him. "They didn't turn out right. I don't think I have a future as a baker or any kind of cook, for that matter."

"You have been trying so many new things lately. Last week, you were sewing dresses. The week before that, you were taking pictures of everything in the house," said Dad. "Is there a reason for all this experimenting?"

"I don't know," Chloe shrugged. "It seems as if everyone else at school is good at something, but I can't sing, or sew, or bake . . . I don't have a talent."

"Oh, Chloe," her dad comforted. "Don't confuse talent with skill. It can take time to learn and sharpen a skill such as baking or sewing, but as for natural talents, God gives everyone something special. Don't give up! You just have to keep trying things."

"I guess you're right," answered Chloe. "Coach Mills said that she would post the results of the soccer team tryouts after school today. Maybe playing soccer will be my talent!"

"That's my girl," Dad said as he wrapped her up in a big hug. "Just keep trying! I'll see you after school."

All through the school day, Chloe tapped her feet nervously under her desk. Even during lunch, she thought back to the soccer tryouts and wondered if she had been good enough to make the team. It was true that she didn't make as many goals as Taylor Springs, but she felt as if she had been a helpful team player the whole week.

At last, the three o'clock bell rang. Chloe grabbed her bag and hurried as fast as she could to the announcement board in the hallway. Many other girls were gathering to see the results as well. Quickly, she spotted the list and read the names silently. She could hear Taylor Springs behind her and some other girls cheering that they had made the team, and she couldn't focus. She read the list again and again as tears began to sting her eyes. There was no Chloe Watson. She hung her head and sneaked away quietly so that no one would see her disappointment, and as she headed down the hallway toward the exit, she let a few of the tears fall.

She stopped for a minute at the cafeteria, sat down at a table, and rested her head on her arms. *Just keep trying* . . . she repeated her dad's words to herself. Then she began to think out loud, "But I'm tired of failing! I don't want to feel like this anymore!"

"Hey, you're good!" a voice behind her interrupted.

Embarrassed that someone had heard her thoughts, Chloe wiped her tears away and whipped her head around to see Vivian Adams and Samuel Ortiz holding stacks of papers.

"Is that your audition for the Drama Club?" Vivian asked with sparkling eyes.

"The Drama Club?" Chloe repeated.

"Well, actually, we call it C3 or the Curtain Call Club," Samuel explained. "I was in it last year, and we performed 'Key to the Secret Garden' for the whole elementary school!"

"Oh, I remember that!" Chloe exclaimed. "That looked like so much fun."

"You really should audition! Today, we are reading the script for the play *Castle Confusion*, and I can imagine you as the perfect Lady Isabel," Vivian added, holding out a small stack of papers. "This is the script! Think about it, and if you decide to audition, C3 will be backstage until 3:45. Hope to see you later!"

Vivian and Samuel waved as they made their way to the stage door. Chloe looked over the script in her hands as her heart pounded. Thoughts swirled in her mind. "I'm tired of failing over and over again. I just want to be good at something. It seems as if all I ever do is lose—but if I don't keep trying, I'll never know how it feels to win."

A determined smile spread on Chloe's face. She flipped through the script to find Lady Isabel's lines, and a few moments later, she disappeared behind the stage door.

The next week at three o'clock, Chloe was back at the announcement board holding her breath and reading the cast list along with several other boys and girls who had auditioned. Down the list she read, and her heart pounded faster and faster with each line.

Castle Confusion
CAST

LORD PHILIP . . . . . . Derek Jameson
KING EDWIN. . . . . . . Bryce Flanders
LADY JANE. . . . . Raina Underwood
JESTER . . . . Samuel Ortiz
LORD GEOFFREY . . . . Oscar Mason
LADY ISABEL . . . . . . Chloe Watson
QUEEN CECELIA . . . . Vivian Adams
LADY CHARLOTTE . . . Hope Stratford

A smile started in Chloe's heart and soon covered her entire face. She practically skipped out of the school and all the way to the parking lot where her dad was waiting outside the car for her. When she was close enough, she ran up to him and threw her arms around him. "Dad, I did it!" she cried. "I finally did it!"

Time to Think

1. What activities had Chloe tried before joining the C3?

2. What does C3 stand for?

I WONDER . . .

1. Which elements of a narrative did you find in this selection? Explain your answers.

2. Chloe's dad is a one-dimensional character. What main personality trait do you see in him?

3. What purpose does Chloe's dad serve in the story?
   a. to grow and change   b. to move the plot forward

4. Which type of character is Vivian? Explain your answer.
   a. one-dimensional   b. multidimensional

5. How is Chloe Watson a lifelike character?

THINK ON THESE THINGS

God's Word promises that there will be rewards for those who don't quit. Sometimes rewards are gifts that we receive, but most of the time, they are unseen. Satisfaction, joy, knowledge, and achievement can't always be seen, but they are rewards that can be felt and enjoyed by those who persevere.

"And let us not be weary in well doing: for in due season we shall reap, if we faint not." —Galatians 6:9

MEET THE CAST

"Yes, Your Majesty"—oh hi! Sorry, I was busy practicing my lines for my drama club's next play. My name is Chloe Watson. It's nice to meet you! Oh, you like my red cloak? Thanks, it's part of my costume. I like to practice my lines in my costume as much as possible because it helps me get in character.

Ever since I joined my school's drama club, I've been interested in both writing and acting. I love pulling characters out of my mind and putting them on paper. I also enjoy taking characters off the printed page and bringing them to life.

Some characters are multi-dimensional and true-to-life, and I like to show how they grow. Others are one-dimensional, and I work hard to make their major characteristics evident to the audience. Lately, our cast has been studying characters to see what authors do to make them come to life. Then we apply what we've learned to our work. Are you interested in writing and acting too? Take a look at some of the notes of mine and my fellow cast members Vivian and Samuel! You can find them throughout this book. We'll see you soon!

IN THE SPOTLIGHT

❖ DRAMA ❖

ACT, SCENE, CAST, AND STAGE DIRECTIONS

A **drama** is another name for a play or story that can be acted out in front of a group of people. A play is divided into **acts**, and acts are divided into **scenes**. Acts and scenes often change when the characters or setting (location or time) changes.

The **cast** of a play is the people who are chosen to perform the parts of each of the characters. Although the characters' names are printed in the play script, they are usually set apart and are not meant to be read aloud. A play is written much differently from stories or poems. When you are reading a play, you usually read only the narration and the dialogue between the characters out loud. You may see other notes inside parentheses ( ) called **stage directions**. Stage directions tell the cast how to act or where to move while they read their characters' lines. These extra notes help the reader to better understand what is happening in each scene.

EXAMPLE: KING EDWIN: *(leaning his ear toward Philip)* Who?

In this line, King Edwin is the character and *(leaning his ear toward Philip)* tells the cast member how to act. Only the word *Who?* would be read out loud by the cast member playing King Edwin. Let's practice while we read and perform the play *Castle Confusion*.

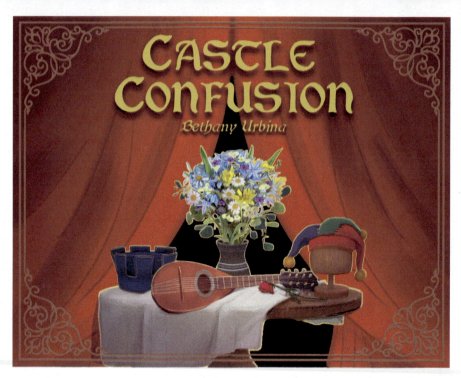

Castle Confusion

Bethany Urbina

༄ Characters ༄
···· Cast List ····

LORD PHILIP ____Ch_____

KING EDWIN ____Ch_____

LADY JANE ____C_____

JESTER ____Ellie_____

LORD GEOFFREY ____C_____

LADY ISABEL ____Ellie_____

QUEEN CECELIA ____Ellie_____

LADY CHARLOTTE _____R_____

---

lord—*a man of authority or rank whom the king places in charge of a portion of land in his kingdom*
lady—*a woman of nobilty or rank; wife, daughter, or sister of a lord*
jester—*a performer who entertained the royal court by joking*

Act 1

Scene 1

(King Edwin paces slowly through his throne room. Lord Philip enters and approaches the king.)

LORD PHILIP: You sent for me, Sire?

(The king continues pacing and does not notice Lord Philip. Philip moves closer to the king and taps him on the shoulder hesitantly.)

KING EDWIN: *(startled, shouting)* What! Who goes there?

LORD PHILIP: It is I, Your Majesty, Lord Philip.

KING EDWIN: *(leaning his ear toward Philip)* Who?

LORD PHILIP: *(louder)* Lord Philip, Your Majesty! You sent for me!

KING EDWIN: Ah yes! My apologies, Lord Philip, my eyesight is not what it used to be.

(enter Lady Jane carrying a tea tray)

LADY JANE: Tea, Your Majesty?

KING EDWIN: *(still facing Philip)* Three what?

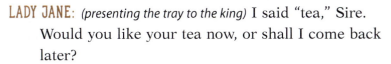

LORD PHILIP: *(to himself)* It seems your hearing is not what it used to be either.

LADY JANE: *(presenting the tray to the king)* I said "tea," Sire. Would you like your tea now, or shall I come back later?

KING EDWIN: Now is perfect, my dear. Thank you.
(Lady Jane prepares and pours the tea while the king continues.)
Now, what was it you wanted to ask me, Lord Philip?

LORD PHILIP: Actually, Sire, I believe you wanted to ask me something.

KING EDWIN: Is that so? *(scratches beard for a moment)* Oh yes, I remember! I need a nobleman to rule over the new estate at Huffley and perhaps marry our castle's own Lady Isabel, for I have promised her father that I would find her a suitable husband.

LADY JANE: *(holding out a teacup)* Be careful, Your Majesty!

KING EDWIN: *(impatiently)* Of course, I will be careful! The dear old man has entrusted me with his daughter's future! I would not just give her hand and the Huffley estate to some jokester!

LADY JANE: *(bowing)* I only meant be careful with the tea, Your Majesty. It is quite hot.

(Lady Jane exits.)

LORD PHILIP: Not to worry, Your Majesty! I know just the man! I would trust him with my own life, and he is rather fond of Lady Isabel, as well. I will send for him to meet you at once.

KING EDWIN: Thank you, Philip. Any man that you recommend will, I am sure, be the perfect man for Huffley.

(Lord Philip exits. King Edwin sips his tea then falls asleep in his chair.)

⋯⋯⋯ Scene 2 ⋯⋯⋯

(In the hall, Lady Jane carries the tea tray toward the kitchen as the jester approaches.)

LADY JANE: *(grabbing the jester's arm)* Oh, you must be our new jester. You have arrived just in time. His Majesty is in a terrible mood this morning. Hurry in quickly and do something to lighten his spirits!

JESTER: *(giving an exaggerated bow)* I assure you, if anyone can bring a smile to the face, warmth to the heart, a laugh to the belly, it is I, my Lady!

LADY JANE: For your sake, Sir, I hope so, and do speak loudly. The king is quite hard of hearing.

(Lady Jane exits toward the kitchen as the jester enters the throne room.)

Scene 3

(The king is asleep in his chair. The jester approaches.)

JESTER: *(taking his hat off his head and bowing)* Your Royal Majesty! It is a pleasure to be in your presence this morning! What shall please my king? A riddle? A song? A play perhaps?

(The king awakens and rubs his eyes.)

Whatever you wish I shall do, Your Majesty!

KING EDWIN: *(standing)* Oh, you must be the man my Lord Philip recommended! Wonderful! *(shaking the jester's hand)* Sir, I hear you are a man of great character.

JESTER: Oh yes, Sire! I have performed many different characters which people love to see. Which role do you wish for me to play?

KING EDWIN: *(leaning toward the jester)* What was that?

JESTER: *(louder)* Which role shall I play for you, Your Majesty?

KING EDWIN: Ah yes! If you are willing, I would like you to be the lord of the Huffley estate and husband to Lady Isabel.

JESTER: I am afraid, Your Majesty, that I am not familiar with that role, but I shall play whichever part I can to make my king smile.

(Jester throws hat to the side and strikes a proud pose. Then he begins to sing.)

I am Lord of Huffley,
Courageous and Wise,
And some ladies say, "A treat for the eyes."
Far and wide they fear my sword,
But Isabel's hand is my true reward.

KING EDWIN: *(chuckling and thumping the jester on the back)* Good man! *(calling offstage to Lady Jane)* Tell Lady Isabel to prepare to meet her fiancé!

JESTER: *(breaks character and gulps)* Fiancé? Wait! Your Majesty, I do believe there has been a mistake!

KING EDWIN: Steak! What a wonderful idea for the marriage feast! I will ask our cook to begin preparing it at once.

JESTER: No, Sire! I am trying to say that I am only a jester!

KING EDWIN: What?

JESTER: *(loudly)* I am a jester!

KING EDWIN: Oh, Chester is it? Lord Chester of Huffley!

(The king exits.)
(Jester frantically hurries after him.)
(Lord Geoffrey enters.)

LORD GEOFFREY: *(bowing)* Lord Philip sent for me, Your Majesty . . . Your Majesty?

(Lord Geoffrey looks around at the empty room, scratches his head, and exits.)

106

Act 2

Scene 1

(In the grand gardens, attendants are bustling back and forth preparing a tea party for the queen. The king strolls by with a frantic jester not far behind.)

JESTER: But Sire, please! I never dreamed you were serious! I cannot truly rule over an estate such as Huffley!

KING EDWIN: Dear Lord Chester, what humility! I have full confidence in you. After all, you come highly recommended by my Lord Philip!

JESTER: I do, Your Majesty?

(Lady Isabel enters the garden with a tablecloth for the tea table.)

KING EDWIN: *(squinting at Isabel)* Ah, Isabel, is that you?

LADY ISABEL: *(curtseying)* Yes, Your Majesty!

KING EDWIN: Come! Come meet your fiancé! This is the man Lord Philip has appointed to be the ruler of Huffley, Lord Chester!

LADY ISABEL: Welcome, Lord Chester! *(pauses)* Are you feeling well? You look rather pale.

JESTER: *(whispering to Isabel)* I am afraid, my Lady, that I am not the man my king thinks I am.

LADY ISABEL: Such a humble man! I am sure if the king has chosen you, that you will do a fine job at Huffley.

KING EDWIN: Is he not a handsome gentleman, Isabel?

LADY ISABEL: *(blushing)* Well, yes, I suppose. His outfit is . . . colorful, to say the least. He must be from the West.

KING EDWIN: The best? Yes! That is just what I said. Nothing but the best for Lady Isabel. *(taking the jester's arm)* Now off we go! We have much to prepare! Good day, Lady Isabel!

107

(King Edwin drags the jester offstage by the hand.)

(Lady Isabel rubs her neck nervously, spreads the tablecloth, then exits the stage.)

Scene 2

(The queen enters the garden and examines the party setup.)

QUEEN CECELIA: *(calls offstage)* Charlotte, these flowers look wilted. Have the gardener cut some fresh roses for the table.

(Lord Philip and Lord Geoffrey enter and approach the queen.)

LORD PHILIP: *(out of breath)* My queen! I have been looking everywhere for King Edwin. You see, I sent Lord Geoffrey to meet the king this morning, but the king was not in his throne room when Geoffrey arrived.

LORD GEOFFREY: *(holding his hat over his heart)* Philip tells me the king wants a man to govern the Huffley estate, and if it pleases the king, I will gladly accept the position. *(Geoffrey bows to the queen.)*

QUEEN CECELIA: Of course! It is a pleasure to meet you! I do not know why the king would have missed his meeting with you, Lord Geoffrey, but do not give it another thought. I will speak to him for you!

LORD GEOFFREY: You are most kind, Your Majesty!

QUEEN CECELIA: Philip, take this gentleman away at once to prepare for the wedding.

LORD PHILIP: *(bowing)* As you wish, my Queen!

(All exit.)

Scene 3

(Queen Cecelia and her ladies sit around the table in the garden drinking tea.)

QUEEN CECELIA: Good afternoon, ladies! *(sips tea)* What an exciting day this has turned out to be! Isabel, I have just met your husband-to-be. My! Isn't he dashing?

LADY ISABEL: *(puzzled)* Do you really think so, Your Majesty?

QUEEN CECELIA: Yes, and such striking brown eyes!

LADY ISABEL: Brown eyes? *(to herself)* I suppose I might have noticed them had he not been wearing such odd clothing.

LADY CHARLOTTE: And I heard the king say that the man sings most beautifully.

LADY JANE: Well then, Isabel! *(giggling)* This Lord of Huffley is sure to serenade you before long.

(All ladies laugh.)

LADY CHARLOTTE: It seems Lady Jane and I are the only ones who have not met this man. Tell us more! How does he look?

(both Queen Cecelia and Lady Isabel speaking at the same time)

QUEEN CECELIA: Well, he looked dark and strong . . .

LADY ISABEL: He looked quite thin and pale actually . . .

(All ladies look at each other with confusion.)

QUEEN CECELIA: *(pauses, then laughs)* You will have to forgive me, Isabel. My old eyes must have deceived me. *(standing)* Oh, to be young like you beautiful ladies! Isabel, let us go prepare for your wedding.

(Isabel and the queen exit.)

LADY JANE: *(beginning to clear the table)* I have not known the queen to have poor eyesight. Have you?

LADY CHARLOTTE: *(shaking out the tablecloth)* No. In fact, just this afternoon, she spotted a wilted rose on the table. It seems to me that she sees perfectly well.

(Ladies exit.)

Act 3

(It is the evening of the wedding. Lord Geoffrey paces outside the church while Lord Philip stands by.)

(Queen Cecelia enters with King Edwin.)

KING EDWIN: *(waving his hands in frustration)* I tell you, Cecelia, I have already been acquainted with the groom!

QUEEN CECELIA: But Lord Geoffrey told me that you were not in the throne room when he arrived!

KING EDWIN: What? Who is Lord Geoffrey?

(Lord Geoffrey steps forward.)

LORD GEOFFREY: *(bowing with his hat over his heart)* I am, Your Majesty!

KING EDWIN: *(squinting at Geoffrey)* Uh . . . How do you do? *(King shakes Lord Geoffrey's hand and then turns to Cecelia.)* This Lord Geoffrey is not the groom! Lord Chester is the groom!

LORD GEOFFREY: *(dropping his hat in surprise)* But Your Majesty! I—

LORD PHILIP: *(interrupting)* Lord Chester, Sire? I have never heard of such a man.

KING EDWIN: What do you mean? You sent him to me!

LORD PHILIP: My King! I sent Lord Geoffrey to meet you. Who is Lord Chester?

(Jester is pushed onstage by guards.)

KING EDWIN: *(squinting at the jester)* Who goes there?

JESTER: *(In frustration, the jester places his jester hat roughly on his head.)* It is I, O King! The jester!

KING EDWIN: Ah, here he is! *(turning to the others)* You see? This is Lord Chester!

(Lady Isabel and her attendants, Lady Jane and Lady Charlotte, enter.)

QUEEN CECELIA: *(shakes her head and says loudly)* Edwin, my dear! This man is the new jester! Not Lord Chester!

KING EDWIN: *(angrily)* A jester!

LADY ISABEL: *(gasping)* I am to marry a jester?

(Isabel swoons—begins to faint. The attendants comfort and fan her.)

KING EDWIN: *(angrily)* Is this one of your games, Jester? Deceiving your king and the ladies of the court?

JESTER: *(dropping to his knees)* No, Sire! I tried to tell you, but I am afraid there has been a misunderstanding. I am only a jester sent for your entertainment by Lady Jane.

(The jester covers his head nervously and braces himself for the king's punishment.)

LORD PHILIP: *(gesturing to Lord Geoffrey)* Your Majesty, this is the man I have appointed for the Huffley estate. He is Lord Geoffrey, and you will find no better match for Lady Isabel.

KING EDWIN: *(pauses then speaks to Lord Geoffrey)* My good man, do you wish to rule over Huffley?

LORD GEOFFREY: If my King so chooses!

KING EDWIN: *(leans his ear toward Geoffrey)* What was that?

LORD GEOFFREY: *(louder)* Yes, my King!

KING EDWIN: *(to the jester)* And you, Lord Chester, I mean— you wish to be simply a jester?

JESTER: Yes, Sire! It is what I do best.

KING EDWIN: *(The king chuckles to himself and helps the jester to his feet.)* Well then, let us not waste another moment! This is a day of celebration! *(guiding Lord Geoffrey to Lady Isabel)* Jester, send our bride and groom off with a song!

JESTER: As you wish, Sire!

(clears throat and sings)

We all knew that Isabel
One day would marry well,
But alas, that is no role of mine.
I am no Lord Chester
But a marvelous jester
And this character suits me just fine.

(All laugh.)

Hurrah for Lord Geoffrey,
The new ruler of Huffley!
Hurrah for his beautiful wife!
May they be happy
And ever speak clearly.
Hurrah for their new wedded life!

ALL: Hurrah!

(All enter the church as curtains close.)

112

Time to Think

1. What is the difference between the characters and the cast? Give examples.

2. Why are the three acts necessary for this plot?

3. What is the author's purpose for *Castle Confusion*?
   a. to entertain
   b. to inform
   c. to teach a lesson

I WONDER . . .

1. The king is a one-dimensional character. Which of the king's physical characteristics accomplish the author's purpose?

2. Which of the characters in this play is the most true-to-life? How can you relate to this character?

3. Why was it important to the action of the play that Lady Jane not see the man that the king thinks is to be the new lord of Huffley?

4. Although the king is very serious when he states, "I would not just give her hand and the Huffley estate to some jokester!" the statement is amusing. Why?

5. What did the king mean when he said, "I hear you are a man of great character"? What did the jester mean when he said that he had "performed many characters"?

STAGE DIRECTIONS

Hi! I'm Vivian. I hope you enjoyed *Castle Confusion*! As president of the C3, that play will always be one of my favorites because it was the first play of the year for our cast and crew. I always find the stage directions to be very helpful. Stage directions are exactly what the name suggests—directions for what to do on stage! The playwright, or author, includes stage directions to help actors reveal important character details to the audience. For example, the stage directions that have King Edwin leaning toward people or squinting at them show the audience that he has hearing and vision problems. The stage direction that has Lady Isabel swoon (my favorite part) reveals her shock at the idea of marrying a jester.

When you're preparing for a play, it's best to read through the entire script a couple of times, stage directions included. I like to highlight each character's directions in different colors. That way, I know who's supposed to be doing a particular action at a particular time. Reading through the entire script before practicing helps me picture my character as a person. By seeing the actions my character performs, I can get a better idea of her personality. For Queen Cecelia, I tried to portray her as someone who is patient and kind but can make things happen. By focusing on Queen Cecelia's personality, I determined good facial expressions to use throughout the play, even when I didn't have specific stage directions.

If you want a little bit of practice with stage directions, pick one character and go back through the play. Focus on that character's stage directions, not just his dialogue. What do the directions reveal about that character's personality? What would you do if you were portraying that character?

To focus on Creative Collaboration, see pages 274–276.

Character

Siera Weber

The play's the thing! It's such a thrill
To have an actor's role.
Just save your acting for the stage,
Or else you'll lose control.

When you play roles outside the stage—
You'll stretch the truth a bit.
Though sorrow follows lives of lies,
Still, acting's hard to quit.

A mask of myth to hide your flaws,
A cloak of pretty lies,
Glitt'ring guile,[1] and gilded[2] good
Make up deceit's disguise.

It might be nice to make believe,
But know before you start:
True character is worn within—
Apparel[3] of the heart.

[1] **guile**—*planned deceit to achieve a goal*
[2] **gilded**—*exaggerated; made out to be better than it really is*
[3] **apparel**—*clothing*

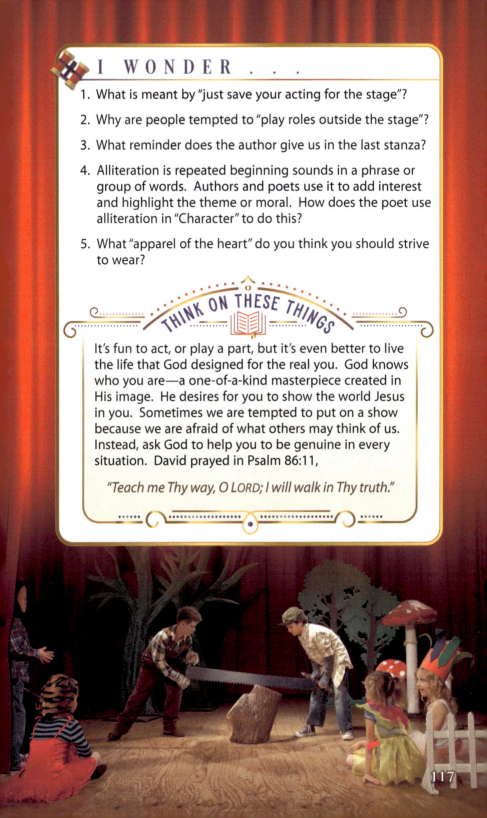

I WONDER . . .

1. What is meant by "just save your acting for the stage"?

2. Why are people tempted to "play roles outside the stage"?

3. What reminder does the author give us in the last stanza?

4. Alliteration is repeated beginning sounds in a phrase or group of words. Authors and poets use it to add interest and highlight the theme or moral. How does the poet use alliteration in "Character" to do this?

5. What "apparel of the heart" do you think you should strive to wear?

THINK ON THESE THINGS

It's fun to act, or play a part, but it's even better to live the life that God designed for the real you. God knows who you are—a one-of-a-kind masterpiece created in His image. He desires for you to show the world Jesus in you. Sometimes we are tempted to put on a show because we are afraid of what others may think of us. Instead, ask God to help you to be genuine in every situation. David prayed in Psalm 86:11,

"Teach me Thy way, O LORD; I will walk in Thy truth."

The Case of the Poetic Pranks: Part One

Siera Weber

Lucas Miller, the lead (and only) investigator of Miller's Mystery Management Agency, sauntered[1] across the parking lot. His best friend, Marcos Rodríguez, waited at the foot of the steps leading to Solid Rock Christian Academy. "What's with the hat, Lucas?"

With a dramatic sigh, Lucas stopped, frowned at Marcos, and proudly straightened his deerstalker cap—a replica of Sherlock Holmes's famous hat. "Remember? Miller's Mystery Management is now open for business. People have to know that I'm a detective if they're going to bring me cases."

"Why don't you make business cards?" Marcos asked as the boys walked up the steps.

Cocking his head to the side, Lucas pondered the suggestion. "That's not a bad idea."

"Yeah, that's what Sylvie's been doing."

Lucas paused. "The new girl?"

"Yeah. She started passing out business cards last Friday." Once the boys stepped into the school, Marcos started rifling[2] through his backpack, sending crumpled papers tumbling to the floor. "Here."

---

[1] **sauntered**—*strolled; walked at a leisurely pace*
[2] **rifling**—*digging through*

Lucas took the card and examined it. It was a bright pink color—*not very professional,* he thought—with the words *Smith's Sleuthing Services* embossed[3] on the front. "Hmm." He tossed the card back to Marcos. "Too glittery."

Marcos shrugged and shoved the card back into his backpack. "Maybe, but it's better than nothing."

Lucas straightened his shoulders and raised his chin. "I don't *need* business cards. People can tell I'm a real detective."

"Oh yeah? How many cases have you solved?"

"Well—none *yet,* but I just need the clients[4] first."

Marcos raised his eyebrows. "Sylvie said that she solved *three* at her old school."

Lucas said nothing, but a feeling of concern tugged at him. *That new girl is trying to steal my career!*

The boys headed to the library, where early students waited until their classrooms were opened. The first person Lucas saw was Sylvie Smith. He wrinkled his nose in disgust and quickly moved to a table on the other side of the room. Perplexed, Marcos followed him. "You okay?" he whispered.

"Mmmhmm." Lucas sat down and pulled out his math book. Marcos followed suit, glancing occasionally at his friend's darkened expression.

"Hey, do you like solving mysteries?"

Lucas glanced up at the question. Sylvie had walked over to his table, and she was looking at his deerstalker cap. Lucas sat up straighter and raised his chin slightly.

---

[3] **embossed**—*raised from the rest of the material as part of a design or pattern*
[4] **clients**—*customers*

120

"Yes. I'm a private investigator."

"Cool! Me too!" Sylvie grinned.

Drawing his eyebrows together, Lucas examined Sylvie. She didn't *look* like a detective. With her regular clothes and pink and yellow notebook, she looked like an ordinary student. *Amateur,* he thought to himself. Out loud, he said, "Well, good luck solving mysteries around here. Nothing ever happens." He didn't want her looking for any cases; she could end up stealing some of his!

"I don't know about that," Sylvie smiled. "Life is usually more exciting than we expect."

Lunchtime proved Sylvie's statement. The students shuffled down the buffet line, filling their trays and talking among themselves. The hum of conversation was interrupted suddenly by Kelsey Blaine's scream from the far end of the line.

All heads turned to Kelsey, who was staring in horror at a mound of mustard that had buried her burger. A few people snickered.

"Ha! That's what you get for using mustard," Tony Walker said from the other side of the table. He reached for a ketchup bottle, shook it once, and tipped it. To the shock of Tony and everyone around him, the ketchup bubbled in the half-empty bottle and rose rapidly, rushing out like a red waterfall and drowning his burger.

"That's crazy!" Theo Briggins, a notorious[5] mischief-maker, grabbed another mustard bottle and shook it.

---

[5] **notorious**—*known widely and unfavorably*

He started to tip it over his plate then, reconsidering, dumped it over Kaitlyn Wilson's plate. Just as with the previous two bottles, a stream of sauce submerged Kaitlyn's hamburger, and she yelled at Theo in dismay.

By this time, Mrs. Lewis, the head cook, had hurried over. "No one use the condiments for now," she called to the cafeteria. She fastened a reproving[6] eye on Theo and said, "You'll be seeing Mr. Riley later today." With a dramatic sigh, Theo trudged to his seat; three weeks into a fresh school year, and he was already a regular visitor to the principal's office.

The cafeteria buzzed with excited whispers as students finished filing through.

"That is the weirdest thing," Marcos said as he and Lucas sat at a table.

Lucas straightened his deerstalker cap. "Yeah, it is." He scanned the room for any possible clues. He happened to see Sylvie at the end of the buffet line. She had set her plate down and was reading a note card, her brow furrowed[7] in a quizzical expression.

I wonder what she found.

At four o'clock, the after-school Writers Club met in their usual location, Miss Greyson's classroom, to brainstorm ideas for their biweekly[8] elementary newspaper.

"Should we cover the ketchup story?" Kaitlyn Wilson asked.

---

[6] **reproving**—*disapproving*
[7] **furrowed**—*wrinkled*
[8] **biweekly**—*every two weeks*

"What's to cover?" Marcos asked. "We don't know what happened."

"I think someone put baking soda in the bottles," Sylvie said.

All heads turned to her, and she continued, "My brothers would do that as a prank when our bottles ran low. Both ketchup and mustard contain vinegar that reacts with baking soda, and the carbon dioxide they produce makes the liquids bubble out."

Lucas narrowed his eyes. Sylvie sure seemed to know a lot about baking soda and condiments. *And she said that life is more exciting than we expect,* he mused.[9] *It was almost as if she knew something would happen.*

Sylvie opened her pink and yellow notebook and pulled out a ketchup-stained note card. "I found this on the buffet line today."

Everyone clustered around her, straining to see. She read it aloud:

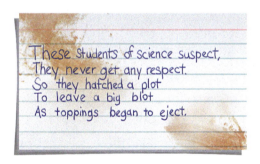

These students of science suspect,
They never get any respect.
So they hatched a plot
To leave a big blot
As toppings began to eject.

The note then passed from hand to hand so that everyone could examine it. After Jamar Wilkes, the club's head editor, glanced at it, he said, "Maybe we could type a short report and put this note at the end. We can ask Miss Greyson about it tomorrow just to make sure."

---

[9] **mused**—*thought carefully*

With that decided, the group tossed around other ideas for the school newspaper. Everyone contributed, except for Kelsey, who was sitting in melancholy silence.

"What's wrong, Kelsey?" Jamar asked finally.

With a sad sigh, Kelsey pulled out the essay she had written for English class. "I don't feel like much of a writer today." She held up the paper, which was covered with red pen.

Sylvie nodded compassionately. "I know it's hard, but teachers mark things to make us stronger writers."

"I know," Kelsey sighed. "It just stings sometimes."

"Whoa, look at all that red!" a voice exclaimed behind them. The members turned around to see Robert Riley, the principal's son, striding into the room.

"Aren't you supposed to be at basketball practice?" Marcos asked.

"I have a few more minutes. I have a newspaper suggestion. What if you guys run a poll about new club ideas? It's pretty boring to just have Science Club, Drama Club, and Writers Club—no offense."

"What kind of clubs?" Jamar asked.

"Maybe a geography club? Or an outdoor recreation club for hiking and stuff."

"Why don't you just make those suggestions to your dad?" Sylvie asked.

Robert sighed. "I already did, but he said the administration and faculty didn't want to add any new clubs yet. But maybe if they saw that there was a lot of student interest, they'd change their minds."

Jamar nodded thoughtfully. "We'll think about it and ask Miss Greyson."

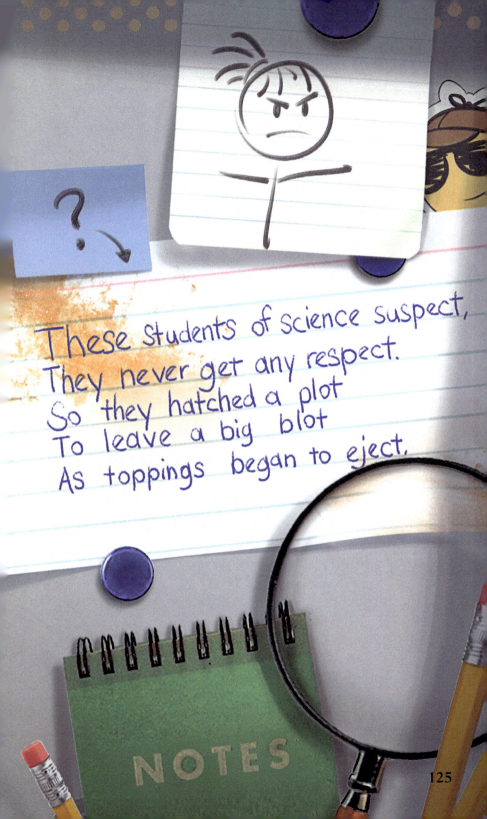

These students of science suspect,
They never get any respect.
So they hatched a plot
To leave a big blot
As toppings began to eject.

"Thanks." Robert turned to leave, but then paused. "What's that?" he asked, pointing to the note that Lucas now held in his hands. Lucas handed it to him.

"Huh, that's weird," Robert said. Handing the note back, he added, "It almost sounds like the Science Club." He checked his watch and then hurried off to basketball practice.

Lucas examined the note. *These students of science*—yes, that certainly sounded like the Science Club. But would they leave a note turning themselves in? That didn't make sense! On the other hand, the Science Club *did* sometimes meet in the cafeteria. Besides, who else would know about the reaction between baking soda and vinegar?

Lucas glanced at Sylvie, who was frowning to herself and scribbling notes in her pink and yellow notebook. He narrowed his eyes. She had known about the baking soda reaction. And she was the one who had "found" the note.

Is this how you solved mysteries at your old school, Sylvie? He thought. *Did you* create *them?*

One thing was for sure, he wasn't going to let his rival get away with *any* mischief.

The next day, Lucas arrived early to school. As he strolled to the library, he kept a sharp eye out for any suspicious activities. Specifically, he kept an eye out for Sylvie Smith.

On his way past Miss Greyson's door, Lucas nearly bumped into Theo, who was exiting the classroom.

"What are you doing?" Lucas asked, narrowing his eyes. None of the students were allowed to be in the classrooms before the teachers opened them.

Theo held up a trash bag. "Mr. Riley said I had to help take out trash and clean the classrooms as punishment for yesterday. I don't get what the big deal was. I didn't know for sure that mustard would spill all over Kaitlyn's plate."

Lucas rolled his eyes.

"Fine, don't believe me!" Theo exclaimed. "I just don't get why I'm in trouble. Mr. Riley should be looking for whoever put baking soda in the bottles."

Lucas's eyebrows flew up. *How would Theo know about that?* "Baking soda?" he asked, trying to keep his voice casual.

"Yeah." Theo smirked for a moment, then paused, shifting from one foot to the other. "It's an old trick. I used to do it all the time at home. When I was like— *seven*." He shrugged. "I guess it's the best some people can come up with."

Interesting.

Bored with the conversation, Theo went to the next classroom, and Lucas started walking to the library. But a thud behind him made him whirl around, only to see Sylvie Smith leaning down and picking up her pink and yellow notebook. *Where did she come from?* He hadn't heard her at all—she seemed to be quite stealthy.

"Hey," Sylvie said, her face reddening with embarrassment.

Is she embarrassed? Lucas asked himself. *Or does she feel guilty for something?*

Later, in English class, Miss Greyson's students were poring over their grammar books, searching for the subjects of the sentences. Miss Greyson walked over to her desk to grab her famous red pen when she paused a moment, staring at the black pens in her nearly empty pen mug. Reaching inside, she pulled out a folded strip of paper and quickly read it.

"Would someone care to tell me what this is all about?" Her sharp question shattered the silence. Twenty-three sets of eyes were raised to look at her, but only Lucas's eyes could see the note clearly from his vantage spot in the first row. His eyes widened.

It was another poem!

Time to Think

1. Who is the lead investigator for Miller's Mystery Management Agency?

2. What disturbance occurred at lunchtime?

3. What was discovered on the buffet line?

4. What new evidence was introduced at the end of part one?

I WONDER . . .

1. Lucas suspected that Sylvie had tampered with the condiment bottles. Do you think his suspicions are reasonable or not?

2. How has the author used setting, plot, and dialogue to develop Lucas into a realistic, lifelike character?

3. Which characters would you define as one-dimensional that were introduced into the story to further the plot?

4. Predict an ending.

INTERNAL MONOLOGUE

In "The Case of the Poetic Pranks," the author uses a technique called internal monologue, showing the character's thoughts as he thinks them, to develop Lucas Miller's character. Dialogue, the conversation between characters, does not always reveal a character's true thoughts. Internal monologue, however, gives readers a glimpse of one character's real reactions. Readers begin to feel as if they know Lucas because they see how his mind works and how he suspects his rival. We understand what drives Lucas to act the way that he does throughout the story.

In my own writing, I can use internal monologue to reveal my characters' hopes and fears. By using internal monologue, I can show my audience what my character is thinking without having to use dialogue.

129

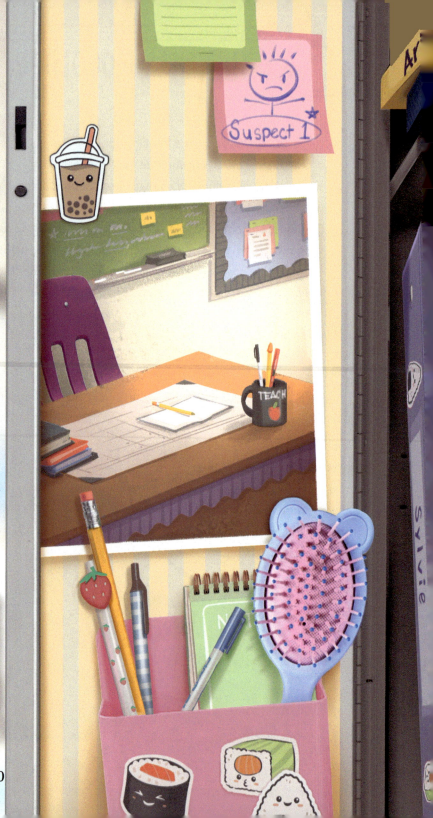

The Case of the Poetic Pranks: Part Two

Siera Weber

When the Writers Club filed into the classroom that Tuesday afternoon, they were whispering among themselves about the disappearance of Miss Greyson's red pens earlier that morning.

"I wish we could have read that note," Marcos whispered.

"Who would do something like that?" Kelsey slumped into her seat, tapping her fingers on the desk nervously.

Miss Greyson's somber-faced entrance put a quick end to the whispering. She stood in front of the club members, looking carefully at each student's face. A few students squirmed uncomfortably under her gaze. Finally, Miss Greyson sighed sadly. "It's a privilege to use the school facilities for after-school clubs. Mr. Riley said that if trouble keeps happening after school, we'll lose that privilege."

The students' jaws dropped. Miss Greyson waited a moment, then added, "I don't want to embarrass anyone. If any of you were involved with hiding my pens or with that cafeteria incident yesterday, speak to me privately after we end tonight."

At that moment, Mrs. Jones, the school secretary, poked her head in and asked for Miss Greyson's help. Miss Greyson handed Jamar the Tuesday agenda and headed out. Propping the door open, she said briskly, "I'll be back shortly."

No one spoke for a moment, then Marcos repeated glumly, "I wish we could have read that note."

The club members tried to focus on the newspaper, but no one had much motivation. After a few unproductive minutes passed, Lucas noticed something on the floor beside Miss Greyson's desk. He stood and picked it up, his eyes widening as he read it. Whirling around to face the class, he waved the note with a dramatic flourish. After clearing his voice, he began to read:

> For students whose greatest delight
> Is only getting to write,
> We *fear* the RED PEN
> And want to know when
> Its marks will be out of our sight.
> — XXXXX

All eyes turned to Kelsey, whose face turned as red as a tomato. "Don't look at me! I know I was complaining yesterday, but I'd never steal anything from a teacher!"

Lucas nodded thoughtfully. *That was a good point.*

Squinting at the piece of paper, Sylvie tapped her pencil against her chin thoughtfully. "Lucas, may I see that for a second?"

For a moment, Lucas felt as if his arm were locked in place. He couldn't bear to hand the note to Sylvie. He

132

didn't want her mishandling evidence. However, with no good reason to refuse, he finally relinquished[1] the note.

"Hmm—this one's typed." Sylvie tapped her pencil again.

Lucas shrugged. "So?"

"I think it's someone—or a couple people—from our grade," Sylvie continued.

"What makes you say that?" asked Jamar.

"Miss Greyson grades a lot of written assignments. Maybe the culprit[2] thought she would recognize his handwriting, so he typed a note here. He wouldn't have to worry about the note in the cafeteria because he figured Miss Greyson wouldn't see it. Or—maybe there are two pranksters, and one wrote the cafeteria note and one typed up the red pen note."

Stunned, Lucas nodded in agreement but then remembered that Sylvie was trying to steal his case, and he cleared his throat. "Well, that's an interesting theory, but—"

"Why would someone do that?" Kelsey blurted out, interrupting Lucas. "And why would they blame us?"

Narrowing her eyes, Sylvie stared into the distance. "I'm not sure yet." She started flipping through her notebook. "There's something more to this—I just can't remember—"

Glaring at his rival,[3] Lucas plopped into a seat and folded his arms. *She seems to guess quite a lot from just two pieces of paper—almost as much as someone who wrote the notes would know.*

At that moment, Miss Greyson returned, glancing carefully around the room. After seeing that nothing appeared

---

[1] **relinquished**—*gave up; surrendered*
[2] **culprit**—*a person guilty of wrongdoing*
[3] **rival**—*competitor*

to be out of place, she gave an approving nod. "I need a couple of volunteers to go interview the elementary basketball team for a sports highlight."

Sylvie immediately raised her hand. "I'll go!"

Lucas narrowed his eyes. Leaving Sylvie—with all of her suspicious behavior—alone, roaming the hallways? That did not seem like a prudent[4] idea. His hand shot into the air. "Me too!"

Miss Greyson nodded. "All right. Take Marcos too, so there are three of you. Go directly to the gym—don't stop by any classrooms."

"Yes, ma'am," they answered, gathering their supplies and hurrying out the door.

Sylvie was still flipping through her notebook when they sat on the bleachers. All through practice, she was distracted. Lucas sighed to himself. *She volunteers for the assignment and doesn't even take notes on the practice.* At one point, he noticed that Sylvie dog-eared one of her pages. Apparently she had found what she had been looking for.

At the end of practice, Coach Gillis let the Writers Club reporters interview the players. Lucas and Marcos had to ask most of the questions; Sylvie was too distracted. When the interviews were finished, Coach Gillis escorted everyone out of the gym, with the writing students following behind.

"I think something's going to happen tonight," Sylvie whispered to Lucas.

---

[4] **prudent**—*wise; having good judgment*

He looked at her sharply. *How could she possibly know that?*

As if reading his mind, she continued. "Whoever's doing this wants to ruin the after-school club program. So far the Drama Club hasn't been implicated[5] in anything."

As the students entered the atrium to wait for their rides, Theo suddenly exclaimed, "Aw man, I left my jacket in the locker room!"

Coach Gillis frowned. "I told you boys to collect everything before we left."

"I'm sorry, I forgot," Theo whined. "Can I just go get it real fast? Before Mr. Davis locks up the gym?"

Coach Gillis hesitated, then Robert Riley said, "I'll go with him, Coach."

Coach Gillis nodded. "Go ahead." As the boys hurried down the hallway, Coach shook his head and started for the front desk to sign students out as their parents picked them up.

As soon as Coach Gillis walked away, Sylvie hurried down the hallway. Shocked, Lucas and Marcos ran after her.

"What are you doing?" Lucas exclaimed. Suspicion flashed through his brain like a bolt of lightning. "Are you the one causing the trouble?"

"No!" she whispered fiercely. "But think about it: who knew about the baking soda? And who complained about the after-school clubs?"

---

[5] implicated—*connected to wrongdoing*

"Ooooh," Marcos said, eyes widening as understanding dawned.

Sylvie stopped in front of Mr. Riley's door and knocked.

The administrator poked his head out. "What's going on, kids?"

"Could you come with us to the gym, Mr. Riley?" Sylvie asked.

The puzzled principal nodded and followed the three students to the gym. Upon reaching the doors, Mr. Riley threw them open and strode in. As the students set their feet over the threshold, they heard Mr. Riley exclaim, "What are you two doing?"

Hanging their heads, Robert and Theo stood at the end of the gym, their arms full of basketballs. Theo shifted on his feet and was about to speak, but Mr. Riley held up his hand. "I think you two need to come to my office." He turned to the three students behind him. "I'd like to chat with you as well, but that can wait until tomorrow."

The next day, Lucas noticed that neither Theo nor Robert were in class. For a moment, satisfaction filled him—the culprits were caught. The next second, his satisfaction vanished. *Sylvie* had solved the case—he hadn't. His shoulders drooped in defeat. How could he call himself a detective?

At the start of Writers Club that afternoon, Miss Greyson told Marcos, Sylvie, and Lucas that Mr. Riley would like to speak to them. The trio hesitantly approached Mr. Riley's office, glancing at each other apprehensively.[6]

---

[6] apprehensively—*anxiously*

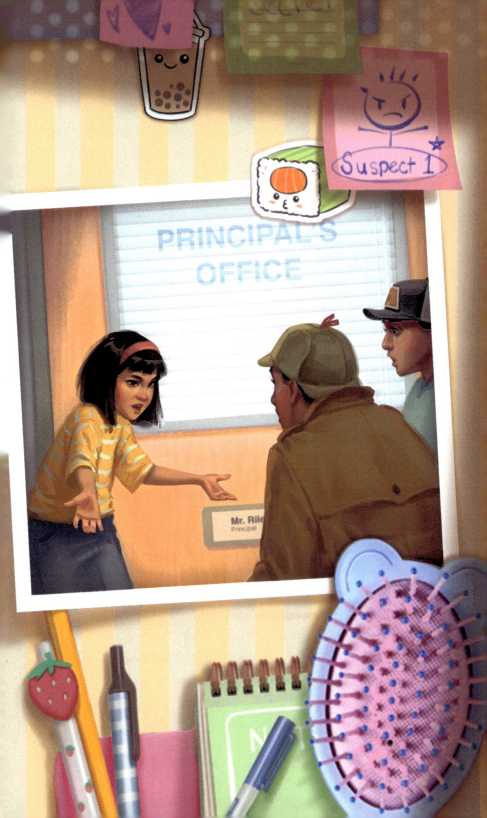

"Come in," Mr. Riley called in answer to Marcos's knock.

The trio slipped in and sat in the chairs Mr. Riley motioned to. He leaned forward on his desk and clasped his hands, his eyes moving from one face to the next.

"Were any of you involved in the recent pranks?" he asked.

"No, sir," Marcos said quickly, and Lucas and Sylvie shook their heads.

"How did you know what was going on last night?"

Sylvie cleared her throat. "We didn't know for sure; it was just a hunch. We'd seen some suspicious behavior from Theo and Robert. Theo told Lucas that he had done a prank with condiments and baking soda before, and he was in Miss Greyson's class before school started the day that her pens went missing. It would have been easy for him to slip them into a trash bag and put the note in their place."

"All right," Mr. Riley said. "But how does that explain Robert's involvement?"

"That was a little trickier, but I've noticed that he and Theo hang out a lot. And one day during Writers Club, Robert came in and mentioned that he really wanted to start new clubs because he didn't like the options the school offers. And he was the one who suggested that the Science Club may have done the condiment crime. I thought maybe—well," she faltered, unsure if she should continue.

"Go on," Mr. Riley nodded, his face serious but still kind.

"They knew that if trouble kept happening after school, you'd cancel all the clubs. I thought that maybe if they couldn't have the club they wanted, they wanted to ruin clubs for everyone."

Whoa. Lucas stared at Sylvie. *She's pretty good*, he admitted to himself—begrudgingly.[7]

Mr. Riley leaned back in his chair and nodded slowly. "That does make sense. Both boys admitted to their actions last night, but they didn't tell me why they did it." He shook his head sadly. "I'm very disappointed. But," he added, his voice growing a little more chipper, "that is some excellent detective work, Miss Smith."

"It was Lucas too," she said. "He's the one who found the second note. That was the clue that showed the culprits were probably our classmates."

At that, Lucas's heavy mood lightened, and he sat up a little straighter.

"Well, thank you to both of you. And you, too, Marcos," Mr. Riley added with a slight grin.

Marcos shrugged. "I was just along for the ride."

Mr. Riley chuckled. "Well, that's all I needed. You're dismissed."

When the trio reached the library, Sylvie paused outside the door and held out her hand to Lucas. "Good work, Detective."

Lucas hesitated, then slowly reached out and shook her hand. "Good work to you too—Detective."

---

[7] **begrudgingly**—*reluctantly; unwillingly*

 Time to Think

1. What observations did Sylvie make about the two notes that had been discovered?

2. What was Lucas's reaction to Sylvie's observations?

3. Who were the culprits?

4. What clues pointed to the actual pranksters?

5. How did Sylvie show wisdom in the way she confronted the culprits?

6. How did Lucas's attitude toward Sylvie change at the end of the story?

 I WONDER . . .

Theo and Robert were aware that their actions would result in consequences, but the consequences that resulted were different from the ones they had hoped for. Explain the difference.

When does a harmless trick cross the line into an unacceptable prank that hurts your reputation and harms someone else?

First, consider the relationship that you have with the person you plan to prank. Do the two of you have a history of doing harmless but silly things that you both enjoy? Could the trick you pull harm him in some way or hurt his feelings? Is it just silly fun, or will your prank set your friend up for ridicule? Ephesians 4:32 commands us to be kind to one another. Any prank that is mean-spirited or harmful is not a harmless trick.

Next, ask yourself if the prank is meant to deceive. God's Word is very clear about honesty. You might think, "I'm not telling any lie when I trick my friend." You can be dishonest without saying a word. In fact, sometimes deceit is acting out a lie rather than telling one. Romans 12:17 reminds us, "Recompense (pay back) to no man evil for evil. Provide things honest in the sight of all men."

The culprits were both mean-spirited and dishonest in the pranks they pulled. Because they were not interested in any of the after-school clubs that were available, they hoped to spoil the enjoyment of the other students by getting their clubs canceled. Their notes dishonestly pointed the finger at certain clubs as if the members of those clubs were the ones behind the pranks. Their behavior was neither kind or honest.

In this fictional story, the pranksters were caught; if the story were true, we would hope the characters learned a valuable lesson. Although this story was entertaining, it gives us the opportunity to think about treating others in a way that honors God.

MYSTERIES

Hey, friends! Samuel here. After reading "The Case of the Poetic Pranks," I was inspired to write my own mystery. Want to join me? Before we can begin, we need to understand how to write this type of narrative!

In mystery stories, the actions and motives of characters drive the plot. By developing convincing characters, you can create a fascinating mystery. There are three main categories of characters you need to consider when writing your story.

THE MAIN CHARACTER

Who is the person solving the case? Is he an experienced detective who knows how to hunt for clues? Or is he just a regular person who accidentally walked into a case that needs to be solved? Knowing your main character's experience will help you decide what types of clues he discovers and how he discovers them. What motivates your main character? Does he want to solve the case to get credit, or does he want to solve the case to help someone else? Your main character's motivation will affect how he notices the correct clues.

THE CULPRIT

Who committed the crime? What was his motivation? Knowing the culprit's motive will help you determine what clues to place in your story. Is your culprit proud and confident? He might make a comment that gives the main character a clue. Is your culprit smart and secretive? The main character might notice him sneaking away or catch him hiding important evidence. Sometimes, your culprit might not even be a true villain. Maybe he "stole" someone's bag, but only because it looked exactly like his! By figuring out your culprit's personality and motivations, you can leave good clues for your readers to follow.

THE DISTRACTION

A mystery becomes even more interesting when you have distracting hints that point to other characters who end up being innocent. It helps if your distracting character has a possible motive for committing the crime. If you choose to add distracting hints in your story, remember to balance them with real clues. You want to keep your readers in suspense, but you also want them to have a chance to solve the mystery with you.

To write your own Mystery, see page 277.

IN THE SPOTLIGHT

❧ POINT OF VIEW ❧

A very important feature of any story is the speaker, or narrator. As you read a selection, you are viewing the events of the story through the eyes of the **narrator**. The narrator is not the same as the author of the story. The narrator himself may be a character within the story, or the narrator may tell events that happened to other characters. Point of view describes the narrator's perspective, or the viewpoint from which the story is being told.

If the story is told in the **first-person point of view**, the narrator includes himself as a character in the story by using first-person pronouns such as the words *I*, *me*, *my*, or *we*. Because the narrator is a character himself, his knowledge will usually be limited to the knowledge of the character within the story.

Third-person point of view is used when the narrator does not refer to himself and is not included as a character within the story. He will use third-person pronouns such as *they*, *he*, and *she* or proper names, and his knowledge of the story may be unlimited.

 Time to Think

Choose the point of view that describes each statement.
   a. first-person   **b.** third-person

1. The narrator is not a character in the story.

2. The narrator refers to himself as *I* in the story.

Identify which stanzas are written in first- or third-person point of view. Explain your answer.

THE RHINO

I found a rhino on my lawn,
And I called out, "Hey you, be gone!"
Then with his mighty, pointed snout,
From my own house he chased me out
And stole my couch to sit upon!

A chap called Charlie had a lawn
That he found a rhino on.
He yelled, "Get lost!"
But at what cost?
The rhino's there, but Charlie's gone.

BALLOONS

Each day I sing a merry tune,
For nothing fills my heart with fear.
Not sharks, nor bears, nor huge typhoons—
Can interrupt my spirit's cheer.
Well—perhaps I spoke too soon—
There is one thing I won't go near.
I must admit: I fear balloons.

A girl named Carla had no fear
Of sharks, nor bears, nor huge typhoons.
She took on spiders with great cheer
And always sang a merry tune.
But then her courage disappeared
The day she saw a big balloon.

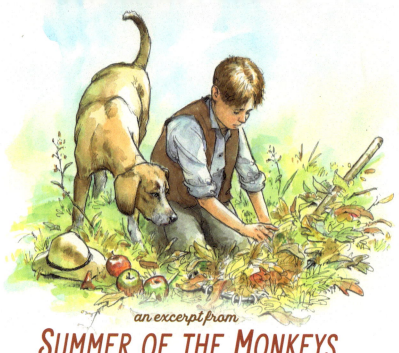

an excerpt from

SUMMER OF THE MONKEYS

Wilson Rawls

Monkeys do not live in the Ozarks. That's what fourteen-year-old Jay Berry Lee thought when he spied a little monkey high in the treetops. Jay Berry had been sent to the river bottoms[1] to find his family's wandering cow when he saw that unlikely sight. He told his grandpa, proprietor[2] of the country store and Jay Berry's unfailing supporter, and Grandpa had the answer. A circus train had derailed a few miles away, and all the monkeys had escaped. Many had been rounded up by the circus folk, but about thirty monkeys remained at large. Jay Berry could hardly believe his ears when he heard of the princely sum being offered for their safe return—two dollars for each of the small monkeys and one hundred dollars for the big monkey. With his grandpa's help, he concocts a plan to capture the monkeys and earn the reward. *Summer of the Monkeys* is set in the late 1800s in what is now the state of Oklahoma; this selection describes the main character's first attempt as a monkey wrangler.

[1] **bottoms**—*low lands beside a river*
[2] **proprietor**—*owner and manager*

146

It was almost sunup when I arrived at the hole Papa and I had dug. I opened my net and very carefully placed it on the ground with about a foot of the handle and the celluloid³ rings sticking over the rim of the hole. Then I started covering the handle, loop, and netting with dead leaves and grass.

After everything had been completely covered, I placed three big apples in the center of the hidden loop and then backed off to one side to see what kind of a job I had done.

I was very pleased with my net-hiding skill. "Rowdy," I said, "I don't know much about trapping this way, but you'll have to admit one thing, that net is sure hidden."

Even if Old Rowdy couldn't understand some of the things I did, he always acted like he did anyway. He wagged his tail and seemed to be pleased with everything.

Picking up my sack, I said, "Come on, boy, let's get in the hole and wait for those monkeys."

With Rowdy behind me, we got down on our stomachs, squirmed back under the brush, and dropped down in the hole.

Rowdy and I hadn't been in the hole ten minutes when from somewhere in the bottoms an old woodpecker started banging away on a dead snag. This seemed to wake up everything in the bottoms. Birds started chirping and squirrels began chattering. From across the river, a big old bullfrog started drumming away—brro-o-m, brro-o-m.

"Rowdy," I whispered, "if those monkeys are around, I don't think it'll be long now. Nothing could sleep with all that racket going on. I hope they're hungry and would like to have a few apples for breakfast."

---

³ **celluloid**—*the first manmade plastic material*

When I first heard the noise, I couldn't make out what it was—although I knew that I had heard it before. It was a slow, scratchy, leaf-rattling noise. Then I noticed that the brush over the top of the hole started shaking.

"Rowdy," I whispered, "something is messing around with the brush up there. You don't suppose it could be that smart monkey?"

Then I saw what it was. It was a big, old, black snake as big around as my arm. There was no doubt but what he had just shed his skin because he was as black and shiny as a new stove pipe. On he came, sticking out his tongue and twisting his way through the brush. When he was directly over the top of the hole, he stopped and peered down at Rowdy and me.

I thought, "Now wouldn't it be something if that snake decided to come down in this hole?"

Things began happening to me. I got as cold all over as I did the time some mean boys threw me in a spring. My skin started crawling around on me. I stopped breathing and my old heart went absolutely crazy.

"Rowdy," I said, in a low voice, "I know that old black snake isn't poison, but he's still a snake. If he takes a notion⁴ to come down in this hole, everything in the bottoms will know that we're down here because I'll probably make a lot of racket."

I wanted to run but I couldn't. The only way out of that hole was right over the snake and I never did like to run over snakes.

Ordinarily Rowdy wasn't scared of snakes; that is, if he was out where he could maneuver around a little. But he didn't seem to like the idea of sharing that hole

---

⁴ **notion**—*a sudden idea*

with the snake any more than I did. He was whimpering and trying his best to crawl under me.

In desperation, I picked up a handful of dirt and threw it in the snake's face. This scared him. He reared his head back, stuck his tongue out at me about a thousand times, then slithered on through the brush and disappeared.

Letting out a lot of air that had long since grown stale, I breathed a sigh of relief and said, "Rowdy, that was close, wasn't it? For a second there, I sure thought we'd have to let that snake have this hole."

The next visitor we had came awfully close to messing up everything. It was a big old hornet. He came buzzing around in the brush and then dropped down in the hole. Gritting my teeth, I closed my eyes, held my breath, and tried to sit as still as a knot on a bur oak tree.

I didn't know why I was holding my breath because I knew that the old saying of how you could hold your breath and nothing would sting you was pure hogwash.[5] I had tried that before and it hadn't worked at all.

Rowdy would have absolutely nothing to do with anything that had wings and stingers. I had taken him on several wasp-fighting expeditions and the little red warriors had really worked him over. He knew all too well that you couldn't hide from them and it was impossible to outrun them. I had to hold onto his collar and squeeze him up tight to keep him from having a runaway.

The hornet buzzed all around us. I just knew that he was looking me over for a good soft spot to jab his stinger in. Finally, after what seemed like hours, he must have decided that there wasn't anything in the hole worth stinging and buzzed on his way.

---

[5] **hogwash**—*nonsense*

Wiping the sweat from my brow, I said, "Rowdy, I've sure learned one thing today. If you want to get everything in these bottoms interested, just dig a hole. That's all you have to do. I wouldn't be a bit surprised if a skeleton didn't come jiggling around next."

Everything went all right for the next thirty minutes, and then I began to have those old doubts again. Maybe Papa was right. Maybe those monkeys had left the country. The more I thought about it, the more convinced I was that my monkey-catching days had come to an end.

I had just about decided to give up and go home when all at once I heard that hundred dollar monkey squall. I perked up like our old hens did when a chicken hawk came flying around.

"Did you hear that, Rowdy?" I whispered. "It was that hundred dollar monkey. We're still in business."

I raised up to where I could peek through the brush and started looking for monkeys. At first I couldn't see a thing. Then I saw one. He was a little brown monkey and was sitting on a stump about thirty feet away.

I was keeping my eyes on him when that big monkey let out another squall. From down in the hole, I couldn't tell where he was, but I knew that he was close-by. Peering up through the brush, I saw him. He was sitting on a low limb of the bur oak tree, directly above my net, looking down at the apples.

I could tell by the big monkey's actions that apples were just what he wanted for breakfast, but he couldn't seem to convince himself that everything was all right.

He stood up on his short legs and started looking things over. Once he looked straight at my hiding place, and I all but crawled down in my skin.

"Rowdy," I whispered, "he's looking for us but I think we've got him fooled this time."

As if he had finally made up his mind, the big monkey squalled again and started moving backward and forward on the limb—all the time uttering those deep grunts.

"Rowdy," I whispered, "he's talking to those little monkeys. I know he is because he did the same thing before. I wonder what he's saying to them this time."

The big monkey must have been telling the little monkeys that everything looked all right to him because here they came. A whole passel[6] of them dropped down from the branches and started grabbing apples.

I couldn't see my net for monkeys. They were standing all over it. Very gently, I took hold of the handle with my left hand and caught hold of the blue ring with my right hand. Using the rim of the hole for leverage, I jerked down on the handle and yanked the blue ring.

Just as I pulled the ring, I heard the big monkey let out a warning cry, but it was too late. The net had already closed.

---

[6] **passel**—*a large number or group*

I couldn't see too well through the brush but I could tell that I had caught something, for the handle of the net was jerking in my hand more than it did when I had Old Gandy wound up in it.

When the net flipped up out of the leaves and grass, it scared the monkeys half to death. Screeching and chattering, they scattered in all directions and disappeared in the timber.

Rowdy and I threw brush all over the bottoms when we came boiling up out of the hole. My eyes all but popped out of my head when I saw that I had caught two little monkeys in my net. I was so pleased I whooped like a possum hunter whooping to his dog.

"I've got them, Rowdy," I shouted. "I got two of them. Look at 'em."

Rowdy was just as pleased as I was. Wagging his long tail, he ran over and started barking and growling at the flouncing[7] monkeys.

The monkeys were so cute and I was so happy that I had finally caught one, I couldn't keep my hands off of them. I wanted to touch one. Working the handle back through my hands until the net was close to me, I poked a finger through the mesh and tickled one in the ribs.

I wouldn't have been more surprised if I had stuck my finger in the firebox of Mama's cook stove. The monkey squeaked and sank his teeth in my finger. I dropped the net and did a little squalling myself.

Slinging my hand and leaping in the air, I shouted, "You bit me. What did you do that for? I wasn't going to hurt you."

---

[7] flouncing—flinging or bouncing about

Rowdy had seen the monkey bite me and he really got mad. He darted in, grabbed one of the monkeys—net and all—in his mouth and started shaking it.

"No, Rowdy, no!" I yelled. "Don't you hurt that monkey."

I yelled too late. It seemed the monkey just turned over in his skin and sank his needle-sharp teeth right in the end of Rowdy's nose.

Rowdy wouldn't have turned loose of a bumblebee any faster than he did that monkey. He bawled and jumped back so fast he almost fell over backwards. Sitting down on his rear, he looked at me and started whimpering.

"Well, don't look at me," I said, "I can't help you. I got bit, too."

It was then that I realized I really had a problem. How was I going to get those monkeys out of the net and into my gunny sack.

"Rowdy," I said, "for all the good this sack is doing us, we may as well have left it at home. I can't get my hands close to those monkeys. They would eat me up."

I decided that I'd just take monkeys, net, and all to the house and maybe Mama and Daisy could help me figure out something.

Holding the net out in front of me as if I were carrying a couple of poison snakes, I started for home. I hadn't gone a hundred yards when the unexpected happened. That hundred dollar monkey dropped down from a syca-more tree and landed smack in the center of the game trail I was walking on. Rowdy and I wouldn't have stopped more suddenly if we had run face on into a white oak tree.

Standing on his short stubby legs and waving his long arms in the air, the big monkey started squalling. He lay down on the ground and rolled over and over. Every little while he would jump up and rush straight at me, showing his teeth, and uttering those deep grunts. He squalled and he screamed. Then he began picking up sticks and chunks and throwing them at me.

Usually when I got scared I could almost outrun my shadow, but I was beyond being scared, I was paralyzed. All I could do was stand there like I was in a trance, hold onto my net, and stare at that big monkey.

Rowdy was between the monkey and me. Every hair on his back was standing straight up. He was growling way down deep and showing his teeth to that squalling monkey.

A full minute went by before it dawned on me that I was still in one piece. When I realized this, I began noticing things. Every time the big monkey ran at me he only came a little way, then he would turn and shuffle back. He was bluffing.[8] I was so sure of it that I got a little of my courage back, but not very much.

"Rowdy," I said, in a croaking voice, "don't jump on that monkey. I don't think he means to harm us. I think he's bluffing, or at least I hope he is."

On hearing my voice, the big monkey went all to pieces. He squalled and here he came shuffling along the ground with his big mouth open and grunting. He came close enough this time to grab the metal loop of my net and start jerking on it.

Every time the big monkey jerked the net his way, I would jerk it back my way. We played tug of war for a few seconds, then he turned his end loose and ran back down the trail a little ways. He lay down in the dirt and

[8] **bluffing**—*frightening or threatening someone with no intent to follow through*

started squalling and screaming and cutting all kinds of capers.⁹ I thought he was having a fit.

All the time this was going on, I had the feeling that the big monkey was trying to tell me something. I tried hard to figure out what it was but I was so scared I couldn't. Just then here he came again, scooting along on the game trail, screaming and making enough racket to scare a person to death. He grabbed my net and started jerking on it again.

It was the same thing all over. We had another jerking session. Again the big monkey turned his end of the net loose, ran back down the trail, lay down, and had another rolling, squalling fit. As I stood there holding onto my net and watching that monkey throw a tantrum, I figured out what it was that he was trying to tell me. He was telling me to turn the little monkeys loose.

"Rowdy," I said, "I believe that silly monkey wants me to turn these little ones loose. But he can just keep on wanting. After all I've gone through to catch them, there'll be whiskers on the moon before I let them go. Why, I'll fight him all over these bottoms."

All at once the big monkey stopped squalling and the bottoms got as still as a graveyard. In the silence, an uneasy feeling came over me. Great big drops of sweat popped out on me. I could almost taste the tension.

Never taking my eyes from that big monkey, I said in a low voice, "Rowdy, I don't like this a bit. I have a feeling that something is going to happen."

I had no more than gotten the words out of my mouth when something did happen. Another monkey dropped down out of nowhere and lit¹⁰ on the ground

---

⁹**capers**—*stunts*
¹⁰**lit**—*landed*

not over ten feet from me. Not making a sound, it just
stood there staring at me.

I was having an eyeball fight with that monkey when
another one came from somewhere and plopped himself
down on the other side of me. The first thing I knew there
was a complete circle of monkeys all around Rowdy and
me. They started walking around us stiff-legged, with their
tails standing straight up, and looking at us sideways.

"Rowdy," I said, "I believe these monkeys are up to something. You've been wanting to jump on them, and from the
looks of things, I think you're going to get the chance."

Old Rowdy wasn't scared. He kept looking at me and
waiting for the "Get-um" sign.

I couldn't stand it any longer. Something had to be
done. I jerked off my old straw hat, threw it at one of

the monkeys, and shouted, "You get away from here. Get now!"

I may as well have been telling Sally Gooden not to jump over the pasture fence. The monkeys didn't even act like they had heard what I said. They just kept circling around and around and around. I could see that the circle was getting smaller and smaller.

I almost unscrewed my head from my neck following those circling monkeys with my eyes.

"Rowdy," I said, "we've got to do something.

Just then that hundred dollar monkey started grunting that monkey talk again. The little monkeys must have understood what he was saying, for they stopped circling us. They just stood there on their spindly legs, staring straight at Rowdy and me with no expression at all on their silly little faces.

This was too much for me. Every nerve in my body was twanging like the "e" string on a fiddler's fiddle. I was trying to figure out which way to run when it happened. A small monkey with a long skinny tail dropped down from a branch directly above me and landed right on top of my head. He grabbed a wad of my hair in all four of his tiny paws; then he leaned over and took hold of my right ear with his teeth. I dropped my net and squalled at the same time.

Shouting, "Get-um, Rowdy!" I reached up with both hands, grabbed that monkey by the tail, and started pulling. It was like pulling on the rubber bands of my beanshooter. The harder I pulled, the longer that monkey seemed to get. I learned something right then. The long skinny tail of a monkey is the best thing in the world to get a good hand hold on.

Closing my eyes and gritting my teeth, I gave a hard jerk on the monkey's tail. Along with a lot of my hair and skin, he came loose.

I was never so mad in all my life.

I still had a good hold on the monkey's tail, and before he could turn around and bite my hands, I started turning in a circle as fast as I could. About halfway in the middle of the third turn I let loose. He sailed out over the bottoms like a flying squirrel and lit in the top of a good-sized bush.

The little monkey didn't seem to be hurt at all. He let out a squeak and hopped down to the ground. For a second he stood on his hind legs and showed his needle-sharp teeth; then here he came again—straight at me—ready for some more fighting.

He hadn't taken over three steps when all at once he fell over backwards. He got to his feet again, took a few more steps, and this time he fell flat on his face. He was so dizzy from that whirlwind I had put him through he couldn't seem to do anything. This tickled me.

I yelled, "How do you like that, you little scoundrel? If you jump on my head again, I'll sling you clear into Arkansas."

My fight with the monkey had taken only a few seconds. During that time, I had been so busy I had completely forgotten about Old Rowdy. On hearing a loud beller[11] from him, I turned to see how he was making out. Boy, did I ever get a surprise.

I saw right away that Rowdy had made a terrible mistake. He was having the fight of his life. He usually enjoyed a good fight, but from the looks and sounds

---

[11] **beller**—*bellow; a loud, deep cry*

158

of things, I didn't think he was enjoying this fight very much. He didn't seem to be making any headway at all.

Rowdy was built just right for good monkey biting and the monkeys had sure taken advantage of this. It looked like every square inch of his hide had a monkey glued to it. His long legs and tail were covered with monkeys. Two of the little scoundrels were sitting right on the top of his head, holding on with all four paws. And they had their teeth clamped on his soft tender ears. More monkeys were lined up on his back like snowbirds on a fence; biting, clawing, and squealing. The hair was really flying.

The monkeys were so quick Rowdy couldn't get ahold of them. Every time he snapped at one, he would wind up with a mouth full of air and no monkey.

I saw right away that if I didn't do something the monkeys were surely going to have a hound dog for breakfast. Looking around for a good whipping stick, I spied one about ten feet away and darted over to get it. The monkeys must have realized what I intended to do, for just as I stooped over to get the stick, a little monkey flew in from somewhere and landed right in the middle of my back.

I forgot all about the stick and was trying to reach around behind me and get ahold of the monkey's tail when another one darted in and latched onto my leg. I was trying to get ahold of that one when another one came squeaking in and bit me on the hand.

In a matter of seconds, I had monkeys all over me. They were biting, clawing, scratching, and squealing. I was hopping all over the place and making more racket than a tomcat with his tail caught in a mouse trap.

Just when things were looking really bad for Rowdy and me, from high in the bur oak tree, the big monkey let out a few grunts and a loud squall. He must have been telling the little monkeys not to eat us completely up—to save a little for the next time—because they turned us loose and disappeared in the underbrush.

Everything had happened so fast, it left Rowdy and me in a daze. I could hardly believe it. One minute we were fighting monkeys all over the place, and the next minute there wasn't a monkey in sight. We just stood there in the silence about twenty feet apart looking at each other.

Rowdy seemed to be more mixed up than I was. He just couldn't believe that a fight like that could have happened so fast and ended so fast.

I looked over to where I had dropped my net. There it was right where I had dropped it; wide open and not a monkey in it. I couldn't believe it. How on earth could the little monkeys have gotten out of the net? My first thought was that the yellow ring had gotten tangled in a bush, and while the monkeys were flouncing and dragging the net over the ground, the net had opened.

I glanced down at the yellow ring and almost jumped out of my shoes. I saw that it had been pulled all right and it wasn't tangled in any bush.

Mumbling to myself, I said, "I'll bet while Rowdy and I were fighting the little monkeys, the big monkey sneaked in and opened the net."

I was still trying to figure out how the monkeys had gotten out of my net when I heard a noise from the bur oak tree. I looked up into the branches. There on a big limb stood the big monkey. He was just standing there looking as proud as a general that had won a war.

When the big monkey saw that I was looking at him, he really made a fool out of himself. Staring straight at me, he started jumping up and down on the limb and uttering those deep grunts. He threw his head back and beat on his chest with his paws; then he opened his big mouth and started laughing. He laughed so loud the bottoms rang with his monkey laughter.

This made me so mad I all but choked.

Shaking my fist at him, I yelled, "You're not such a brave monkey. You sicked[12] those little monkeys on Rowdy and me but you didn't do any fighting. What's the matter? Are you scared? If you'll come down here, we'll fight you all over these bottoms."

___

[12] **sicked**—*set or commanded an attack*

The big monkey must have understood what I said. He stopped laughing, and with a few grunts, he started dropping down from the tree. My hair flew straight up.

"Rowdy," I said, as I picked up my empty net, "I don't know about you but I've had all the monkey fighting I want for one day. Let's get out of here."

I didn't have to tell Rowdy but once. He felt about monkey fighting like I did. He was way ahead of me when we tore out down a game trail.

We hadn't gone far when I looked back over my shoulder and saw that there were no monkeys chasing us.

"Rowdy," I said, as I walked over and sat down on a sycamore log, "I think we can stop running now. Maybe we can't whip those monkeys but we can sure outrun them."

It looks as if the monkeys have triumphed over Jay Berry in his first attempt to capture them and gain the reward money. As he and his faithful hound return home, he voices his discouragement to Rowdy and speculates that perhaps they would be better off if they just left the Ozarks. Will Jay Berry give up for good? Will memories of the monkey battle be too painful for him to make another attempt? Or will the fantastic sum of money for the monkeys' capture tempt him to try once more? How do you think this monkey tale will end? You will want to read the rest of the book to discover how *Summer of the Monkeys* reaches its conclusion.

Time to Think

1. Is this story written in first-person or third-person point of view? *It was*

2. Who is the narrator and what role does he play in the story?

3. How were the smaller monkeys caught? *By Anet*

4. How was the plan to trap the monkeys flawed, and when was the mistake realized? *that the mongs got ont of the net and that he was enBded*

I WONDER . . .

1. A good author knows how to "show" us his characters through their thoughts and actions, and not just "tell" the reader about them. How did the author show us that the main character is wise in the ways of living creatures?

2. How does this author use human characteristics in his description of the big monkey, and what does this say about the way Jay Berry viewed the big monkey?

3. How did the big monkey react to Jay's final challenge, and how did Jay Berry and Rowdy respond?

SHOWING DETAILS

Hi friends!

Vivian here! Let me show you what I'm doing. I had so much fun reading *Summer of the Monkeys*! I wanted to highlight some of my favorite details from the story. I love this book for the humor and especially for the characters. A skillful writer can make a character come to life by showing us his thoughts and actions rather than by simply telling us about the character. In *Summer of the Monkeys*, Wilson Rawls does just that.

When we first meet Jay Berry, he's deep in the Ozark river bottoms, putting his plan to capture the monkeys into action. The author doesn't tell us that his character knows a lot about his surroundings, the creatures that live there, and how to deal with them. Instead, he shows us how his character reacts to the setting by letting us see what he does and how he thinks. Jay creates a trap by digging a pit and carefully placing a net over it; then, he covers the trap with leaves to hide it from the monkeys. He strategically arranges some tempting apples to entice the monkeys to his trap. When the animals in the river bottoms become noisy, the author doesn't need to tell us; instead, the author shows us. He allows us to read Jay Berry's thoughts as he listens and waits, and we hear what he hears— the hammering of the woodpecker, the chattering of the squirrels, and the booming voice of the bullfrog.

Jay Berry's knowledge of the setting and its creatures becomes obvious again when he immediately recognizes that the snake had recently shed its skin and that although it's a potentially dangerous creature, it's not venomous. (Although if I were Jay, I would have been out of that hole and running home in a flash!) He demonstrates his wisdom and his knowledge when he chooses to wait out the hornet while keeping Rowdy as quiet as possible. By showing us these details, the author paints a realistic portrait of a fourteen-year-old boy exploring the natural world of the Ozarks in the late nineteenth century.

Now, let's go to pages 147–148 and highlight phrases the author uses to describe what Jay sees and hears.

IN THE SPOTLIGHT

❧ INFORMATIVE NONFICTION ❧

Sometimes, an author writes to teach a lesson or to entertain readers. At other times, the author's purpose is to provide information. **Informative** texts may appear in a variety of writings—including biographies, how-to manuals, essays, and more. Through these types of text, the author can present information in a variety of ways.

The author may choose to describe a topic by providing details that help you understand something you may know little about. The author could also choose to compare and contrast two different things, using their similarities and differences to help you decide which is best. At times, the author might point out the causes of different events and the effects they had on the world around them. At other times, the author might describe problems and the creative solutions people have used to solve them. When describing a process, an author will often write information in a sequence going from the first step to the final step. And, when relating a historical event or events in a person's life, the author might write in chronological order from the beginning to the end.

Regardless of how the author presents information, his goal is to provide knowledge for you to gain. Identifying the way that the author writes nonfiction selections helps you know how to watch for the most important information. As you read the next selection, determine the author's purpose and watch for the most important information.

Mary Mapes Dodge

Mary Mapes was born into a wealthy and well-educated family living in New York City in 1831. Mary's father was a chemist who studied scientific farming. Although many girls at this time did not receive an extensive education, Mr. Mapes hired private tutors to instruct his daughters in languages, literature, music, and art. Since he believed that most children's literature of that time was not worth reading, he encouraged his children to read from the Bible and William Shakespeare's works. The Mapes were a devoted family, and Mary recalled having a particularly happy childhood. Mary excelled at art, music, and writing. By the time she was a teenager, she was helping her father write pamphlets.

In 1851, twenty-year-old Mary started her own family when she married William Dodge; within a few years they became the parents of two boys. William Dodge died in 1858, leaving his young family in a very bad financial position. Mary was determined to provide for her boys, maintain a loving home for them, and see that they received a good education. She began supporting her family by working as an editor at two of her father's magazines. Soon she was writing short stories as well. In 1864, her stories were published together in a book, *The Irvington Stories*.

The following year, in 1865, Mary published the book for which she would become most famous—*Hans Brinker, or the Silver Skates*. Mary had never been to the Netherlands, but after she read *The Rise of the Dutch Republic*, she became fascinated with the country. Two of her neighbors were a Dutch couple who were immigrants; they were happy to tell her about the customs of their homeland. After she finished the book, Mary showed it to her publisher, who was not enthusiastic about it at all. He told her that no one wanted to read about Holland, especially not children. Reluctantly, he published the book. It was an immediate success in America. Soon it was translated into several other languages, including Dutch; it was a hit in the Netherlands! *Hans Brinker, or the Silver Skates* was awarded the most prestigious prize given at that time for works of literature, the Moynton Prize of the French Academy.

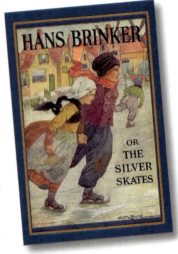

Mary continued her contributions to children's literature when she accepted a job at the weekly paper *Hearth and Home* in 1869. She was put in charge of the household and juvenile departments. Her diligence and talents were noticed, and under her direction, the paper increased in popularity. In 1873, Mary was offered the opportunity to be the editor of *St. Nicholas*, a new magazine designed for children. Her goal was to provide literature for children that would be instructive and entertaining while building good character. Many of the best writers of the day contributed to *St. Nicholas*; among them were Louisa May Alcott, Robert Louis Stevenson, Mark Twain, and Henry Wadsworth Longfellow. Rudyard Kipling contributed a series of stories that later became *The Jungle Book*. A feature of the magazine was St. Nicholas League, which encouraged the magazine's young readers to submit their own writing. Gold and silver badges were awarded, along with cash prizes. A young E. B. White won a prize for an essay he submitted.

Mary Mapes Dodge remained active as an editor until her death at age 74 in 1905. Her work in promoting excellence in children's literature remains her greatest contribution.

 ## Time to Think

1. Where and when was Mary Mapes born?

2. How do you think her early experiences with reading and writing helped prepare her for her later career?

3. What events influenced Mary to become a professional editor and writer?

4. How did Mary Mapes Dodge get her information about the Netherlands, a country she had never visited?

5. What was the public's response to *Hans Brinker, or the Silver Skates*?

6. What was Mary Mapes Dodge's most significant contribution?

 # I WONDER . . .

1. "Meet the Author: Mary Mapes Dodge" was written to _____.
   a. entertain the reader
   b. inform the reader
   c. teach a lesson

2. The author's purpose was to _____.
   a. describe problems and solutions
   b. relate significant events in a person's life
   c. sequence a step-by-step process

an excerpt from

HANS BRINKER, OR THE SILVER SKATES

Mary Mapes Dodge

Hans and Gretel Brinker come from a desperately poor but loving family. Honest and hardworking, the children do all they can to help their mother, who must care for their severely ill father. Like all Dutch children of that day, they have mastered the sport of ice skating, and they enjoy what little free time they have gliding and speeding across the ice. On this morning in early December, Hans and his sister learn of a wonderful race to be held later that month and of the amazing prize to be won by the best skaters.

On a bright December morning long ago, two thinly clad children were kneeling upon the bank of a frozen canal in Holland.

The sun had not yet appeared, but the gray sky was parted near the horizon, and its edges shone crimson with the coming day. Most of the good Hollanders were enjoying a placid[1] morning nap. Now and then some peasant woman, poising a well-filled basket upon her head, came skimming over the glassy surface of the canal; or a robust[2] boy, skating to his day's work in the

---

[1] **placid**—*pleasantly calm; undisturbed*
[2] **robust**—*full of strength; sturdy*

town, cast a good-natured grimace[3] toward the shivering pair as he flew along.

Meanwhile, with many a vigorous puff and pull, the brother and sister, for such they were, seemed to be fastening something on their feet, not skates, certainly, but clumsy pieces of wood narrowed and smoothed at their lower edge, and pierced with holes, through which were threaded strings of rawhide.[4]

These strange-looking skates had been made by the boy Hans. His mother was too poor even to think of such a thing as buying skates for her little ones. Rough as these were, they had given the young Hollanders many a happy hour on the ice; and now as with cold, red fingers our young Hollanders tugged at the strings, their solemn faces bending closely over their knees, no vision of impossible iron runners came to dull the satisfaction glowing within.

In a moment the boy arose, and with a pompous swing of the arms and a careless, "Come on, Gretel," glided easily across the canal.

"Ah, Hans," called his sister plaintively,[5] "this foot is not well yet. The strings hurt me on last market-day, and now I cannot bear them tied in the same place."

"Tie them higher up, then," answered Hans, as without looking at her he performed a wonderful cat's cradle step on the ice.

"How can I? The string is too short."

Giving vent[6] to a good-natured Dutch whistle, the English of which was that girls were troublesome creatures, he steered toward her.

---

[3] **grimace**—*a facial expression showing disapproval*
[4] **rawhide**—*leather; cattle skin*
[5] **plaintively**—*sadly*
[6] **"giving vent"**—*blowing air with force through the lips*

"You are foolish to wear such shoes, Gretel, when you have a stout leather pair. Your *klompen*[7] would be better than these."

Hans had taken a string from his pocket. Humming a tune as he knelt beside her, he proceeded to fasten Gretel's skate with all the force of his strong young arm.

"Oh! Oh!" she cried, in real pain.

With an impatient jerk Hans unwound the string. He would have cast it upon the ground in true big-brother style, had he not just then spied a tear trickling down his sister's cheek.

"I'll fix it, never fear," he said, with sudden tenderness, "but we must be quick; the mother will need us soon."

Then he glanced inquiringly about him, first at the ground, next at some bare willow branches above his head, and finally at the sky, now gorgeous with streaks of blue, crimson, and gold.

Finding nothing in any of these localities to meet his need, his eye suddenly brightened as, with the air of a fellow who knew what he was about, he took off his cap and removing the tattered lining, adjusted it in a smooth pad over the top of Gretel's worn-out shoe.

"Now," he cried triumphantly, at the same time arranging the strings as briskly as his benumbed fingers would allow, "can you bear some pulling?"

Gretel drew up her lips as if to say "Hurt away," but made no further response.

In another moment they were laughing together, as hand in hand they flew along the canal, never thinking whether the ice would bear them or not; for in Holland ice was generally an all-winter affair. It settled itself

---

[7] **klompen**—*Dutch wooden shoes*

upon the water in a determined kind of way, and so far from growing thin and uncertain every time the sun was a little severe upon it, it gathered its forces day by day and flashed defiance[8] to every beam.

Presently, squeak! squeak! sounded something beneath Hans's feet. Next his strokes grew shorter, ending with a jerk. Finally, he lay sprawling upon the ice, kicking against the air with many a fantastic flourish.[9]

"Ha! ha!" laughed Gretel, "that was a fine tumble!" But a tender heart was beating under her coarse blue jacket, and even as she laughed, she came, with a graceful sweep, close to her prostrate[10] brother.

"Are you hurt, Hans? Oh, you are laughing! Catch me now!" And she darted away, shivering no longer, but with cheeks all aglow and eyes sparkling with fun.

Hans sprang to his feet and started in brisk pursuit, but it was no easy thing to catch Gretel. Before she had traveled very far, her skates, too, began to squeak.

Believing that discretion[11] was the better part of valor,[12] she turned suddenly and skated into her pursuer's arms.

"Ha! ha! I've caught you!" cried Hans.

"Ha! ha! I caught *you*," she replied, struggling to free herself.

Just then a clear, quick voice was heard calling, "Hans! Gretel!"

"It's the mother," said Hans, looking solemn in an instant.

By this time the canal was gilded with sunlight. The pure morning air was very delightful, and skaters were

---

[8] defiance—*resistance*
[9] flourish—*showy movement*
[10] prostrate—*lying flat on one's face*
[11] discretion—*carefulness; sense*
[12] valor—*courage*

gradually increasing in numbers. It was hard to obey the summons. But Gretel and Hans were good children. Without a thought of yielding to the temptation to linger, they pulled off their skates, leaving half the knots still tied. Hans, with his great square shoulders and bushy yellow hair, towered high above his blue-eyed little sister as they trudged homeward. He was fifteen years old and Gretel was only twelve. He was a solid, hearty-looking boy, with honest eyes and a brow that seemed to bear a sign "goodness within." Gretel was lithe[13] and quick; her eyes had a dancing light in them, and while you looked at her cheek the color paled and deepened just as it does upon a bed of pink and white blossoms when the wind is blowing.

Nearly all the outdoor work, as well as the household labor, was performed by Hans and Gretel. At certain seasons of the year, the children went out day after day to gather peat,[14] which they would stow away in square, brick-like pieces, for fuel. At other times, when home-work permitted, Hans rode the towing-horses on the canals, earning a few stivers[15] a day; and Gretel tended geese for the neighboring farmers.

Hans was clever at carving in wood, and both he and Gretel were good gardeners. Gretel could sing and sew and run on great, high, home-made stilts better than any other girl for miles around. She could learn a ballad in five minutes, and find, in its season, any weed or flower you could name; but she dreaded books, and often the

[13] **lithe**—*gracefully flexible*
[14] **peat**—*partly decomposed plants*
[15] **stivers**—*old Dutch five-cent coins*

very sight of the figuring-board in the old schoolhouse would set her eyes swimming. Hans, on the contrary, was slow and steady. The harder the task, whether in study or daily labor, the better he liked it.

It was only in winter that Gretel and Hans could be spared to attend school; and for the past month they had been kept at home because their mother needed their services. Raff Brinker, their ill father, required constant attention, and there was black bread to be made, and the house to be kept clean, and stockings and other things to be knitted and sold in the market-place.

While they were busily assisting their mother on this cold December morning, a merry troop of girls and boys came skimming down the canal. There were fine skaters among them, and as the bright medley of costumes flitted by, it looked from a distance as though the ice had suddenly thawed, and some happy tulip-bed were floating along on the current.

Up and down the canal within the space of a half mile they skated, exerting their racing powers to the utmost.

Suddenly the whole party came to a standstill and, grouping themselves out of the way of the passers-by, all talked at once to a pretty little maiden, whom they had drawn from the tide of people flowing toward the town.

"Oh, Katrinka!" cried the girls, "have you heard of it? The race—we want you to join!"

"What race?" asked Katrinka, laughing. "Don't all talk at once, please, I can't understand."

"Why, we are to have a grand skating match on the twentieth. It's all Hilda's work. They are going to give a splendid prize to the best skater."

"Yes," chimed in a half a dozen voices, "a beautiful pair of silver skates—perfectly magnificent! with, oh! such straps and silver bells and buckles!"

"The girls' pair are to have bells," interposed Hilda, quietly, "but there is to be another pair for the boys with an arrow engraved upon the sides."

"Who is to try?" asked Katrinka.

"All of us. It will be such fun! And you must, too, Katrinka. But it's school time now, we will talk it all over at noon."

At noon the children poured forth from the school-house, intent on having an hour's practicing upon the canal.

They had skated but a few moments when Carl Schummel said mockingly to Hilda, "There's a pretty pair just coming on the ice! The little rag pickers! Their skates must have been a present from the king direct."

"They are patient creatures," said Hilda, gently. "It must have been hard to learn to skate on such odd skates. They are poor, you see. The boy has probably made the skates himself."

Hilda sailed past the others and halted beside Gretel. "What is your name, little girl?"

"Gretel, my lady," answered the child, somewhat awed by Hilda's rank, though they were nearly the same age, "and my brother is called Hans."

"Hans is a stout fellow," said Hilda, cheerily, "and seems to have a warm stove somewhere within him, but *you* look cold. You should wear more clothing, little one."

Hans flushed as he saw tears rising in Gretel's eyes. "My sister has not complained of the cold; but this is bitter weather they say"; and he looked sadly upon Gretel.

"It is nothing," said Gretel. "I am often warm, too warm when I am skating. You are good, Miss, to think of it."

"No, no," answered Hilda, quite angry at herself. "I am careless, cruel; but I meant no harm. I wanted to ask you—I mean—if—" and here Hilda, coming to the point of her errand,[16] faltered before the poorly clad but noble-looking children she wished to serve.

"What is it, my lady?" exclaimed Hans eagerly. "If there is any service I can do—any—"

"Oh! no, no," laughed Hilda, shaking off her embarrassment, "I only wished to speak to you about the grand race. Why do you not join it? You both can skate well, and anyone may enter for the prize."

Gretel looked wistfully at Hans, who, tugging at his cap, answered respectfully:

"Ah, Miss, even if we could enter, we could skate only a few strokes with the rest. Our skates are hard wood, you see" (holding up the sole of his foot), "but they soon become damp, and then they stick and trip us."

16 **errand**—*a short trip to accomplish a task*   **177**

Gretel's eyes twinkled with fun as she thought of Hans' mishap in the morning, but she blushed as she faltered out timidly:

"Oh, no, we can't join; but may we be there, my lady, on the great day to look on?"

"Certainly," answered Hilda, looking kindly into the two earnest faces, and wishing from her heart that she had not spent so much of her monthly allowance for lace and finery. She had but eight *kwartjes*[17] left, and they would buy but one pair of skates, at the furthest.

Looking down with a sigh at the two pair of feet so very different in size, she asked:

"Which of you is the better skater?"

"Gretel," replied Hans, promptly.

"Hans," answered Gretel, in the same breath.

Hilda smiled.

"I cannot buy you each a pair of skates. Or even one good pair; but here are eight *kwartjes*. Decide between you which stands the best chance of winning the race, and buy the skates accordingly. I wish I had enough to buy better ones. Good-bye!" And, with a nod and a smile, Hilda, after handing the money to the electrified Hans, glided swiftly away to rejoin her companions.

"Miss! Miss van Gleck!" called Hans in a loud tone, stumbling after her as well as he could, for one of his skatestrings was untied.

Hilda turned, and with one hand raised to shield her eyes from the sun, seemed to him to be floating through the air, nearer and nearer.

---

[17] **kwartjes** (kwart yuh)—*old Dutch 25-cent coins*

"We cannot take this money," panted Hans, "though we know your goodness in giving it."

"Why not, indeed?" asked Hilda, flushing.

"Because," replied Hans, bowing like a clown, but looking with the eye of a prince at the queenly girl, "we have not earned it."

Hilda was quick-witted. She had noticed a pretty wooden chain upon Gretel's neck.

"Carve me a chain Hans, like the one your sister wears."

"That I will, lady, with all my heart. We have whitewood in the house, fine as ivory; you shall have one tomorrow," and Hans hastily tried to return the money.

"No, no," said Hilda decidedly. "That sum will be but a poor price for the chain," and off she darted, outrunning the fleetest among the skaters.

Hans sent a long, bewildered gaze after her; it was useless, he felt, to make further resistance.

"It is right," he muttered, half to himself, half to his faithful shadow, Gretel. "I must work hard every minute, and sit up half the night if the mother will let me burn a candle; but the chain shall be finished. We may keep the money, Gretel."

"What a good little lady!" cried Gretel, clapping her hands with delight. "Now Hans, if mother sends us to town tomorrow you can buy the skates in the market-place."

Hans shook his head. "The young lady would have given us the money to buy skates; but if I earn it, Gretel, it shall be spent for wool. You must have a warm jacket."

"Oh, Hans," she continued with something like a sob, "don't say you won't buy the skates, it makes me feel just like crying. Besides, I want to be cold—I mean I'm real, awful warm—so now!"

Hans looked up hurriedly. He had a true Dutch horror of tears or emotion of any kind, and most of all, he dreaded to see his sister's blue eyes overflowing.

"Now mind," cried Gretel seeing her advantage, "I'll feel awful if you give up the skates. *I* don't want them. I'm not such a stingy as that; but I want *you* to have them, and then when I get bigger they'll do for me. Oh-h! count the pieces, Hans. Did ever you see so many!"

Hans turned the money thoughtfully in his palm. Never in all his life had he longed so intensely for a pair of skates, for he had known of the race and had, boy-like, fairly ached for a chance to test his powers with the other children. He felt confident that with a good pair of steel runners, he could readily distance most of the boys on the canal. Then, too, Gretel's argument was so plausible.[18] On the other hand, he knew that she, with her strong but lithe little frame, needed but a week's practice on good runners to make her a better skater. As soon as this last thought flashed upon him his resolve was made. If Gretel would not have the jacket, she should have the skates.

"No, Gretel," he answered at last, "I can wait. Some day I may have money enough saved to buy a fine pair. You shall have these."

Gretel's eyes sparkled; but in another instant she insisted, rather faintly:

"The young lady gave the money to *you*, Hans. I'd be real bad to take it."

Hans shook his head resolutely as he trudged on, causing his sister to half skip and half walk in her effort

---

[18] plausible—*reasonable*

to keep beside him. By this time they had taken off their wooden "rockers," and were hastening home to tell their mother the good news.

"Oh! *I* know!" cried Gretel, in a sprightly tone. "You can do this. You can get a pair a little too small for you, and too big for me, and we can take turns and use them. Won't that be fine?" and Gretel clapped her hands again.

Poor Hans! This was a strong temptation, but he pushed it away from him, brave-hearted fellow that he was.

"Nonsense, Gretel. You could never get on with a big pair. You stumbled about with these, like a blind chicken, before I curved off the ends. No, you must have a pair to fit exactly, and you must practice every chance you can get, until the twentieth comes. My little Gretel shall win the silver skates."

Gretel could not help laughing with delight at the very idea.

"Hans! Gretel!" called out a familiar voice.

"Coming, mother!" and they hastened toward the cottage, Hans still shaking the pieces of silver in his hand.

On the following day, there was not a prouder nor a happier boy in all Holland than Hans Brinker, as he watched his sister, with many a dexterous[19] sweep, flying in and out among the skaters who at sundown thronged[20] the canal. A warm jacket had been given her by the kind-hearted Hilda, and the old shoes had been cobbled into decency. As the little creature darted backward and forward, flushed with enjoyment, and quite

[19] **dexterous**—*skillful and graceful*
[20] **thronged**—*crowded*

unconscious of the many wondering glances bent upon her, she felt that the shining runners beneath her feet had suddenly turned earth into fairyland, while "Hans, dear, good Hans!" echoed itself over and over again in her grateful heart.

The day of the race has been set for December 20. Because of Hilda's thoughtfulness and Hans's unselfishness, Gretel has new skates and is ready to compete. How do you think the race will end? Did you catch the author's hint at the end of this selection? Although the race is an exciting part of this novel, there is much more to discover in its pages. A lost son is found, a father is restored to health, and good favor finally smiles on the Brinker family. You will want to read this classic tale, written by an American author, which is known as one of the most accurate portrayals of life in the Netherlands of long ago.

Time to Think

1. Describe the story's setting.

2. Why were Hans and Gretel skating on wooden skates?

3. What prizes were to be won at the race?

4. Why do you think Hilda was angry with herself after she suggested Gretel should wear a warmer coat?

5. Why did Hans at first refuse to take Hilda's money, and what made him change his mind?

1. How did the author show us that the brother and sister care deeply for each other?

2. When Hilda gave Hans the money to buy skates, the author described him as *electrified*, which in this sense means shocked, greatly thrilled, or excited. Why was Hans electrified?

3. How would you describe Hans's decision to buy the skates for Gretel rather than for himself?

4. Which of these characters are lifelike or multidimensional?

   a. Carl   c. Hans   e. the mother

   b. Gretel   d. Hilda   f. Katrinka

5. Why did the author include one-dimensional characters in the plot?

6. Write a short paragraph predicting how you think the story will end.

   Well it was varry good and they were strong and they were having fun and Beyny nice to ech other and huny fun or scarry

To focus on Comparing Characters, see page 278.

PIPPI FINDS A SNIRKLE

from *Pippi in the South Seas* by Astrid Lindgren

Astrid Lindgren, a Swedish author, wrote novels, short stories, and plays, as well as dozens of children's books. Her books have been translated into many languages and are popular worldwide.

This selection from *Pippi in the South Seas* was translated from Swedish into English by Susan Beard. Susan Beard was born in Great Britain, and her native language is English. She has used her knowledge of the Swedish language to translate many books. Her goal as a translator is to make the book sound as if it were originally written in English, while remaining true to the plot and the style of the original author.

One morning Tommy and Annika came skipping into Pippi's kitchen as usual and shouted good morning. Pippi was sitting in the middle of the kitchen table with Mr. Nilsson, the little monkey, in her arms and a contented smile on her face.

"Morning," said Tommy and Annika again.

"Can you believe it," said Pippi, in a far-away voice. "Can you believe *I'm* the one who made it up? Me and nobody else!"

"What have you made up?" asked Tommy and Annika. It didn't surprise them in the least that Pippi had made something up because she always did, but they wanted to know what it was. "What exactly have you made up, Pippi?"

"A new word," said Pippi, and she looked at Tommy and Annika as if she had only just seen them. "A brand spanking new word."

"What is the word?" asked Tommy.

"A most excellent word," said Pippi. "One of the best I've ever heard."

"Tell us, then," said Annika.

"Snirkle," Pippi said triumphantly.

"Snirkle," said Tommy. "What does it mean?"

"If I only knew," said Pippi. "The only thing I do know is that it doesn't mean dustbin lid."

Tommy and Annika thought for a while. At last Annika said: "But if you don't know what it means then it's not much use, is it?"

"No, that's what annoys me," said Pippi.

"Who actually thought up from the beginning what words mean?" Tommy wondered.

"Most likely a load of old professors," said Pippi. "And people are very odd, I must say. Think of the words they make up! 'Tongs' and 'plug' and 'string' and stuff. No one has a clue where they get them from. But they haven't bothered inventing 'snirkle,' which is a really good word. How lucky I came up with it! And I expect I'll find out what it means, too."

She contemplated this for a few moments.

"Snirkle! Could it possibly mean the very, very top of a blue-painted flagpole, do you think?" she said uncertainly.

"There aren't any flagpoles painted blue," said Annika.

"No, you're right. In that case I haven't the faintest idea. Could it possibly be the sound you make when you trample in the mud and it comes up between your toes?

Let's give it a try: 'Annika trampled around in the mud and it made the most wonderful snirkle.'" She shook her head. "No, that doesn't work. 'It made the most wonderful shblurp'—that's what it ought to be."

She scratched her head.

"This is getting more and more mysterious. But I'll find out, whatever it is. Maybe you can buy it in a shop? Come on, let's go and ask."

Tommy and Annika had nothing against doing that. Pippi went to find her traveling bag that was full of golden coins.

"Snirkle. Sounds expensive. I'd better take a whole golden coin."

And so she did. Mr. Nilsson hopped onto her shoulder as usual and then Pippi lifted her horse down from the veranda.

"No time to waste," she said to Tommy and Annika. "Let's ride. Otherwise there might not be many snirkles left when we get there. It wouldn't surprise me if the town mayor has already taken the last one."

When the horse came galloping through the streets of the little town with Pippi and Tommy and Annika on its back its hooves clattered so loudly that all the children heard it, and they came out to run happily along beside it because they all liked Pippi very much.

"Pippi, where are you going?" they called.

"To buy a snirkle," Pippi said, and pulled on the reins.

The children stopped running and looked baffled.

"Is it nice to eat?" a little boy asked.

"I should say so," said Pippi, licking her lips. "It's delicious. At least, it sounds like it is."

She hopped off the horse outside a baker's shop and lifted down Tommy and Annika. In they went.

"I'd like a bag of snirkles, please," said Pippi. "The crunchy kind."

"Snirkles," said the pretty assistant behind the counter, stopping to think. "I don't think we've got any."

"You must have," said Pippi. "Surely you can find them in every well-stocked shop?"

"Oh, well then, we've already sold out," said the girl, who had never heard of snirkles but didn't want to admit that her shop wasn't as well-stocked as everyone else's.

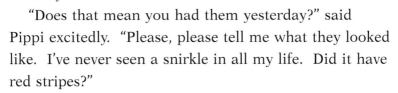

"Does that mean you had them yesterday?" said Pippi excitedly. "Please, please tell me what they looked like. I've never seen a snirkle in all my life. Did it have red stripes?"

The pretty assistant blushed charmingly and said:

"Oh dear, I don't know what they are! But we haven't got them here, anyway."

Pippi walked back to the door, feeling very disappointed. "Then I'll carry on searching," she said. "I'm not going home without a snirkle."

The next shop was an ironmonger's.[1] The assistant bowed to the children politely.

"I'd like to buy a snirkle," Pippi said. "But it must be the very best kind, the kind you kill lions with."

The assistant looked crafty.

"Let me see," he said, scratching behind his ear. "Let me see."

---

[1] **ironmonger**—*British word meaning hardware clerk*

He found a garden rake and held it out to Pippi.

"Will this do?" he asked.

Pippi gave him a withering look.

"That is what educated people call a rake," she said. "But I happened to ask you about a snirkle. Don't try fooling a little innocent child!"

The assistant laughed and said: "We haven't got one of those things you asked for, unfortunately. Try the haberdasher's[2] on the corner."

"The haberdasher's," muttered Pippi. "They won't have one there, I know *that* much."

She looked gloomy for a while but then brightened up.

"Perhaps, when you think about it, a snirkle is an illness," she said. "Let's go and ask the doctor!"

Annika knew where the doctor lived because she had been taken there for her vaccinations.

Pippi rang the bell. A nurse came and opened the door.

"Is the doctor in?" asked Pippi. "It's a very urgent case. A tremendously serious disease."

"Do come in. This way," said the nurse.

The doctor was sitting at his desk when the children came in. Pippi walked straight up to him, closed her eyes, and stuck out her tongue.

"And what is the matter with you?" asked the doctor.

Pippi opened wide her clear blue eyes and pulled in her tongue.

"I'm afraid I've got an attack of the

---

[2] **haberdasher**—*British word for a business that sells small items used for making clothes such as buttons or zippers*

snirkles," she said. "I'm itching all over and my eyelids slam shut when I go to sleep. Sometimes I hiccup. And last Sunday I felt a bit poorly after I'd eaten a bowl of shoe polish and milk. Nothing wrong with my appetite but my food often goes the wrong way so it doesn't do me much good. I must have got an attack of the snirkles. Tell me one thing: is it catching?"

The doctor looked at Pippi's healthy little face and said: "I think you are healthier than most. I'm certain you're not suffering from the snirkles." Pippi grabbed his arm eagerly.

"So there is an illness called that?"

"No," said the doctor. "There isn't. But even if it did exist, I don't think it would give *you* any trouble."

Pippi looked glum. She curtsied deeply to the doctor by way of saying good-bye, and Annika did the same. Tommy bowed. Then they walked back to the horse that was waiting in the doctor's garden.

Not far from the doctor's house was a block of flats three floors high. A window on the top floor was open. Pippi pointed up at the open window and said: "It wouldn't surprise me if there was a snirkle inside there. I'll pop up and have a look."

And quick as a wink she shinned up the drainpipe. When she came level with the window she threw herself headlong into thin air and caught hold of the windowsill. She pulled herself up and thrust in her head.

Two ladies were sitting in the room inside, chatting. Guess how astonished they were to see a redhead suddenly appear above the windowsill, and hear a voice saying: "Just wondering, is there a snirkle in here?"

The two ladies shrieked in horror.

"Heavens above, child, what are you saying? Has someone escaped?"

"That's precisely what I would like to know," said Pippi politely.

"Oh, perhaps he's under the bed?" cried one of the ladies. "Does he bite?"

"Highly likely," said Pippi. "It sounds like he's got a good set of teeth."

The two ladies clung to each other. Pippi scrutinized the room but finally said regretfully: "No, not even a snirkle's whisker. Sorry for interrupting! I thought I'd inquire, seeing as I happened to be passing."

She slid back down the drainpipe.

"Pity," she said to Tommy and Annika. "There's no snirkle in this town. Let's ride home again."

And that's what they did. As they jumped down from the horse outside the veranda Tommy almost trampled on a little beetle that was scuttling along the gravel path.

"Oh, mind the beetle!" shouted Pippi.

All three crouched down to look at him. He was so small. His wings were green and gleamed like metal.

"What a beautiful little thing," said Annika. "I wonder what kind it is?"

"It's not a May beetle," said Tommy.

"Or a dung beetle, either," said Annika. "And not a stag beetle. I really wish I knew what kind it was."

A delighted smile spread across Pippi's face. "I know," she said. "It's a snirkle."

"Are you sure?" asked Tommy doubtfully.

"Do you think I can't recognize a snirkle when I see one?" said Pippi. "Have you ever seen anything more snirkle-like in your life?"

190

Carefully she moved the beetle to a safer place where he wouldn't get trampled on.

"My sweet little snirkle," she said, tenderly. "I knew I'd find one in the end. But how odd. We've been running around town looking for a snirkle and there was one here all the time, right outside Villa Villekulla."

Time to Think

1. Summarize the plot.

> triyng to find a snirkel But cold not find one so thay went all over town and still did not find one and thats all thay wanted so thay sead im not going home intill i find a snirkel then thay cold not find one so thay just went home. when thay got home thay whatever thay und Smark fornd a bessen But thay did not ___ it was and then sead a snirkel

2. How did the lady at the baker's store and the man at the hardware store try to fool Pippi?

I WONDER . . .

1. Do you think the beetle that Pippi called a snirkle already had a name? Explain your answer.

2. Pippi is a fanciful character; it is unlikely you would meet anyone like her. How did the author make Pippi believable for the world in which she lives?

CHARACTERIZATION

Oh, hey there! Don't mind me, I'm just looking for a snirkle. You know, reading *Pippi in the South Seas* always makes me want to go on a fun adventure. Pippi Longstocking is one of my favorite fictional characters because she is so fun and different from any other fictional orphan. The author used her imagination to develop a completely new kind of character. Pippi is especially strong, independent, imaginative, and creative.

Pippi's physical strength is superhuman—like no other ten-year-old girl, or even boy. In one of her adventures, she picked up two grown men and carried them around, one in each hand! Then, she lifted her horse from the veranda to the ground. Can you find another example of her unbelievable strength?

Pippi is also determined and strong willed. You might call her a natural-born leader. In fact, Pippi's friends Tommy and Annika are happy to follow her because they know she will always take them on the greatest adventures. No matter what happens, Pippi's determination causes her to keep trying until she gets the results she's looking for.

Pippi takes care of herself. She lives alone with her monkey, Mr. Nilsson, and her horse. She never needs to think about money because she owns a bag full of gold coins. Pippi has complete freedom to choose what to do and when to do it. Because she is good at everything she does, her adventures always end well.

The author must have a great imagination and a curious mind since she gave those things to Pippi. Pippi's friends were not surprised that she invented a new word: snirkle. Even though she was not sure what a snirkle was, Pippi definitely knew what it was not. After her search took her all over town, she found the snirkle in her own back yard, and she was happy with the results.

Even though Pippi has some unusual abilities, it is easy to imagine that she is real. Maybe it's because we all wish we could be a little like Pippi, or at least have her for a friend. I know I'd like to count her as one of mine!

To focus on Main Character, see page 279.

How to
Draw a Beetle

Some art used in children's literature is simple line drawings in black and white. You may see grays or color added to these line drawings. Follow this step-by-step process below to draw a beetle on a separate sheet of paper.

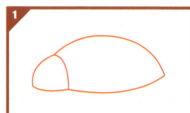

1 First, draw a small, rounded triangle shape for the head and attach a pointed oval for the body.

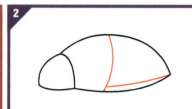

2 Then, draw lines to show wings.

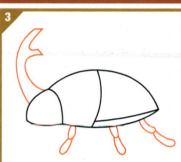

3 Draw curved lines to add the horn and thin oval shapes for each leg.

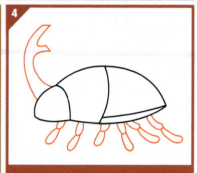

4 Add three more legs each, giving this beetle a total of six!

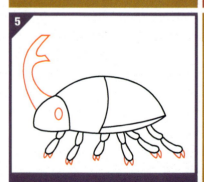

5 Draw a single oval for the eye and two triangular toes for each leg.

6 Color in the eye, leaving a small white oval; add an oval on the shell and some curved stripes for the belly.

194

MEET THE AUTHOR
Jack Prelutsky

The famous poet Jack Prelutsky has some good advice for anyone who wants to be a writer—"always carry a notebook and at least two pens." His interest in the arts began when he was young; at one time he studied music and considered a career as an opera singer. He tried his hand at sculpting, photography, and sketching. A friend suggested he show his drawings to a children's book editor. The editor pronounced his work some of the worst she had ever seen, but she saw promise in the verses he quickly wrote to accompany the sketches. He was encouraged to continue to write, and in 1976, his first volume of poetry, *A Gopher in the Garden and Other Animal Poems*, was published. Since then, he has created over fifty volumes of highly imaginative poetry, intended for children but enjoyed by people of all ages. Prelutsky offered advice to other aspiring writers when he said, "The only limitation is your own imagination."

Time to Think

1. Why do you think Prelutsky gave the advice "always carry a notebook and at least two pens"?

2. How did Prelutsky react to being told his sketches were bad? What can you learn from his reaction?

3. Do you think Prelutsky would have been as successful if he had allowed the words of his editor to discourage him? Explain your answer.

4. What did Prelutsky mean when he said, "The only limitation is your own imagination"?

Be Glad Your Nose Is on Your Face

Jack Prelutsky

Be glad your nose is on your face,
not pasted on some other place,
for if it were where it is not,
you might dislike your nose a lot.

Imagine if your precious nose
were sandwiched in between your toes,
that clearly would not be a treat,
for you'd be forced to smell your feet.

Your nose would be a source of dread
were it attached atop your head,
it soon would drive you to despair,
forever tickled by your hair.

Within your ear, your nose would be
an absolute catastrophe,
for when you were obliged to sneeze,
your brain would rattle from the breeze.

Your nose, instead, through thick and thin,
remains between your eyes and chin,
not pasted on some other place—
be glad your nose is on your face!

Have you ever stopped to think that the position of your fingers and toes and even your nose is intentional? We have so much to be thankful for! Psalm 139:14 says, *"I will praise Thee; for I am fearfully and wonderfully made: marvellous are Thy works; and that my soul knoweth right well."*

IN THE SPOTLIGHT

RHYME SCHEME AND METER

Prelutsky's poetry is known for its use of traditional rhyme schemes. A **rhyme scheme** is the pattern made by the rhyming words found at the end of each line. Letters of the alphabet are used to indicate words that rhyme. Notice the rhyme scheme in "Be Glad Your Nose Is on Your Face." *Face* and *place*, at the ends of lines 1 and 2, rhyme; lines 3 and 4 end with the rhyming words *not* and *lot*. The rhyme scheme of the first stanza is *aabb*. Does the rest of the poem follow this same pattern?

Another feature of most poetry is **meter**, the rhythmic pattern created by the stressed (louder) and unstressed (softer) syllables in a line of poetry. Jack Prelutsky's poetry is known for its strong rhythms. When you exaggerate the stressed syllables, it is easy to hear the meter—"Be glad your nose is on your face." Here we have four pairs of syllables, in which an unstressed syllable is followed by a stressed syllable. Can you hear the same meter in the rest of the poem?

Not all poems have a rhyme scheme or a consistent meter, but many do. Whether you write your own verse, or enjoy reading the poems of others, an understanding of rhyme schemes and meter will add to your enjoyment of poetry.

SOME PEOPLE I KNOW

Jack Prelutsky

Some people I know like to chatter,   *a*
while others speak hardly a word;   *b*
some think there is nothing the matter   *a*
with being completely absurd;[1]   *b*
some are impossibly serious,   *c*
while others are absolute fun;   *a*
some are reserved[2] and mysterious,   *b*
while others shine bright as the sun.   *a*

Some people I know appear sour,
but many seem pleasant and sweet;
some have the grace of a flower,
while others trip over their feet;
some are as still as a steeple,
while some need to fidget and fuss;
yet every last one of these people
is somehow exactly like us.

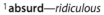

[1] **absurd**—*ridiculous*
[2] **reserved**—*kept to themselves; private*

🟦 I WONDER . . .

1. Summarize the central idea or theme of the poem.

2. When a new rhyme appears within a stanza, the next letters in the alphabet are assigned. Fill in the blanks to complete the poem's rhyme scheme. Does the second stanza follow the same pattern?

3. Does "Some People I Know" have a consistent meter? How do you know?

4. Match the expressions the poet uses to contrast people.

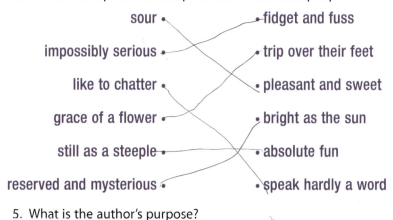

sour • • fidget and fuss

impossibly serious • • trip over their feet

like to chatter • • pleasant and sweet

grace of a flower • • bright as the sun

still as a steeple • • absolute fun

reserved and mysterious • • speak hardly a word

5. What is the author's purpose?

to shw this stdy that he neds   **199**

Especially Serious Sam

Jack Prelutsky

I'm especially serious Sam—
Yes I am! Yes I am! Yes I am!
I have no desire to smile,
Not even once in a while.
My aspect's entirely severe,
I never know laughter or cheer.
Hilarity's not to my taste,
While whimsy is simply a waste.

I'm unsympathetic to fun,
And don't get the point of a pun.[1]
Mere banter[2] I cannot abide,
I haven't a frivolous[3] side.
Don't bother displaying your wit,
I won't be impressed, not a bit.
Jocosity's[4] truly a bore,
And horseplay I wholly abhor.[5]

I'm somber, sedate, and intense,
So merriment doesn't make sense.
Caprice[6] I dismiss and disdain,
It pains my so-serious brain.
You might as well jest[7] with a wall,
A rug or a red rubber ball,
Tell jokes to an oyster or clam . . .
I'm especially serious Sam.

---

[1] **pun**—*a humorous play on words using words that have similar sounds but different meanings*
[2] **banter**—*good-natured joking*
[3] **frivolous**—*silly; fun*
[4] **jocosity**—*joking; humor*
[5] **abhor**—*hate*
[6] **caprice**—*sudden unplanned change in actions or thoughts*
[7] **jest**—*make a joke*

I WONDER . . .

1. What sense does Sam completely lack?

2. Does he wish he had what he lacks? Explain your answer.

3. Why does Sam say that you might as well jest with a wall, a rug, or a ball?

4. How does the author include repetition?

5. What do you think was the author's purpose in writing this poem?

I Went Hungry on Thanksgiving

Jack Prelutsky

I was hungry on Thanksgiving,
but I couldn't eat a thing,
I couldn't eat a drumstick
and I couldn't eat a wing,
I couldn't have the pickles
or the gravy-covered rice,
the pumpkin pie was luscious,
but I couldn't have a slice.
I was starving for some stuffing
or a tasty yellow yam,
or a puffy little muffin
spread with homemade berry jam.
Our dinner looked delicious,
but I didn't dare to touch,
I went hungry on Thanksgiving—
my new braces hurt so much.

I WONDER . . .

How did the poet stir your curiosity and create suspense?

❧ DIALECT ❧

Within a language, there are different ways of speaking called *dialects.* A **dialect** is a variety of a language spoken by people of a certain region or by people who follow a particular occupation. Dialect is more than just the accent you hear when someone speaks. Accent is only one feature of dialect; dialect also includes the speaker's choice of words and his grammar. The English language has many dialects for each of the many areas where English is spoken. A person in the United States speaks with a different dialect than someone from Great Britain. Their accents would be different, and they would also make different word choices. The American would call the front and back sections of a car the hood and the trunk. The Briton would call them the bonnet and the boot. People living in the same region who have different cultures or upbringings would also speak with different dialects.

When the author has the character speak in a certain dialect, it helps the reader to imagine and understand a little bit more about the character and the setting. For example, if a character says, "G'day, Mate!" one might guess that he is from Australia, but if the character says, "Hey, y'all!" he is probably from the Southeastern United States.

You can often spot dialect because of unusual spelling or contractions. If you see words that are shortened or pushed together and joined with apostrophes, the character might be speaking in dialect. In the selection "We Are Seven," look for these types of changes, especially in Mr. Cobb's speech.

WE ARE SEVEN

from *Rebecca of Sunnybrook Farm*
by Kate Douglas Wiggin

In this excerpt, we meet Rebecca Randall, a girl growing up in rural Maine just as the author herself did. Like
Kate, Rebecca faces poverty and hardship after the death
of her father. Now everyone says that her chance for a
good education, provided by her aunts, will "be the making" of her. Can Rebecca tame her extravagant imagination and learn to fit in with the ways of her humorless
Aunt Miranda? Today we come upon Rebecca as she
opens a new chapter in her life and makes a new friend.

The old stage coach was rumbling along the dusty
road that runs from Maplewood to Riverboro. The day
was as warm as midsummer, though it was only the
middle of May, and Mr. Jeremiah Cobb was favoring the
horses as much as possible, yet never losing sight of the
fact that he carried the mail. The hills were many, and
the reins lay loosely in his hands as he lolled[1] back in
his seat and extended one foot and leg luxuriously[2] over
the dashboard. His brimmed hat of worn felt was well
pulled over his eyes.

There was one passenger in the coach—a small dark-
haired person in a glossy buff[3] calico[4] dress. She was
so slender and so stiffly starched that she slid from
space to space on the leather cushions, though she
braced herself against the middle seat with her feet and

---

[1] **lolled**—*sat or rested in a relaxed manner*
[2] **luxuriously**—*in a very comfortable manner*
[3] **buff**—*brownish-yellow; tan*
[4] **calico**—*a light cotton fabric with a small, busy printed pattern*

extended her cotton-
gloved hands on each
side, in order to maintain
some sort of balance.
Whenever the wheels
sank farther than usual
into a rut, or jolted suddenly over a stone, she
bounded involuntarily
into the air, came down
again, pushed back
her funny little straw

hat, and picked up or settled more firmly a small pink
sunshade, which seemed to be her chief responsibility,—
unless we except a bead purse, into which she looked
whenever the condition of the roads would permit,
finding great apparent satisfaction in that its precious
contents neither disappeared nor grew less. Mr. Cobb
guessed nothing of these harassing details of travel, his
business being to carry people to their destinations,
not, necessarily, to make them comfortable on the way.
Indeed he had forgotten the very existence of this one
unnoteworthy little passenger.

When he was about to leave the post-office in Maplewood that morning, a woman had inquired whether
this were the Riverboro stage, and if he were Mr. Cobb.
Being answered in the affirmative, she nodded to a child
who was eagerly waiting for the answer, and who ran
towards her as if she feared to be a moment too late.
The child might have been ten or eleven years old perhaps, but whatever the number of her summers, she had
an air of being small for her age. Her mother helped

her into the stage coach, deposited a bundle and a bou-quet of lilacs beside her, superintended[5] the "roping on" behind of an old hair trunk, and finally paid the fare, counting out the silver with great care.

"I want you should take her to my sisters' in River-boro," she said. "Do you know Mirandy and Jane Sawyer? They live in the brick house. She's going there, and they're expecting her. Will you keep an eye on her, please? If she can get out anywhere and get with folks, or get anybody in to keep her company, she'll do it. Good-by, Rebecca; try not to get into any mischief, and sit quiet, so you'll look neat an' nice when you get there. Don't be any trouble to Mr. Cobb.—You see, she's kind of excited.—We came on the cars from Temperance yesterday, slept all night at my cousin's, and drove from her house—eight miles it is—this morning."

"Good-bye, mother, don't worry; you know it isn't as if I hadn't traveled before."

The woman gave a short laugh and said in an explanatory way to Mr. Cobb, "She's been to Wareham and stayed over night; that isn't much to be journey-proud on!"

"It *was traveling*, mother," said the child eagerly and willfully. "It was leaving the farm, and putting up lunch in a basket, and a little riding and a little steam cars, and we carried our nightgowns."

"Don't tell the whole village about it, if we did," said the mother, interrupting the reminiscences[6] of this expe-rienced voyager. "Haven't I told you before," she whis-pered, in a last attempt at discipline, "that you shouldn't

---

[5] **superintended**—*directed*
[6] **reminiscences**—*recalling of memories*

talk about nightgowns and stockings and—things like
that, in a loud tone of voice, and especially when there's
men folks round?"

"I know, mother, I know, and I won't. All I want to say
is"—here Mr. Cobb gave a cluck, slapped the reins, and
the horses started sedately[7] on their daily task.

Mrs. Randall watched the stage out of sight, gathered up
her packages from the bench at the store door, and stepped
into the wagon that had been standing at the hitching-post.
As she turned the horse's head towards home she rose to
her feet for a moment, and shading her eyes with her hand,
looked at a cloud of dust in the dim distance.

---

[7] **sedately**—*calmly and quietly*

"Mirandy 'll have her hands full, I guess," she said to herself; "but I shouldn't wonder if it would be the making of Rebecca."

All this had been half an hour ago, and the sun, the heat, the dust, the contemplation of errands to be done in the great metropolis of Milltown, had lulled Mr. Cobb's never active mind into complete oblivion[8] as to his promise of keeping an eye on Rebecca.

Suddenly Mr. Cobb heard a small voice above the rattle and rumble of the wheels and the creaking of the harness. At first he thought it was a cricket, a tree toad, or a bird, but having determined the direction from which it came, he turned his head over his shoulder and saw a small shape hanging as far out of the window as safety would allow. A long black braid of hair swung with the motion of the coach; the child held her hat in one hand and with the other made ineffectual attempts to stab the driver with her microscopic sunshade.

"Please let me speak!" she called.

Mr. Cobb drew up the horses obediently.

"Does it cost any more to ride up there with you?" she asked. "It's so slippery and shiny down here, and the stage is so much too big for me, that I rattle round in it till I'm most black and blue. And the windows are so small I can only see pieces of things, and I've most broken my neck stretching round to find out whether my trunk has fallen off the back. It's my mother's trunk, and she's very choice of it."

Mr. Cobb waited until this flow of conversation had ceased, and then said jocularly:—"You can come up if you want to; there ain't no extry charge to sit side

---

[8] **oblivion**—*being unaware of surrounding circumstances*

208

o' me." Whereupon he helped her out, "boosted" her up to the front seat, and resumed his own place.

Rebecca sat down carefully, smoothing her dress under her with painstaking precision, and putting her pink parasol[9] under its extended folds between the driver and herself. This done she pushed back her hat, pulled up her white cotton gloves, and said delightedly:

"Oh! this is better! This is like traveling! I am a real passenger now, and down there I felt like our setting hen when we shut her up in a coop. I hope we have a long, long ways to go?"

"Oh! we've only just started on it," Mr. Cobb responded genially;[10] "it's more 'n two hours."

"Only two hours," she sighed. "That will be half past one; mother will be at cousin Ann's, the children at home will have had their dinner, and Hannah cleared all away. I have some lunch, because mother said it would be a bad beginning to get to the brick house hungry and have Aunt Mirandy have to get me something to eat the first thing.—It's a good growing day, isn't it?"

"It is, certain; too hot, most. Why don't you put up your parasol?"

"Oh dear no! I never put it up when the sun shines; pink fades awfully, you know, and I only carry it to meetin' cloudy Sundays; sometimes the sun comes out all of a sudden, and I have a dreadful time covering it up; it's the dearest thing in life to me, but it's an awful care."

At this moment the thought gradually permeated[11] Mr. Jeremiah Cobb's slow-moving mind that the bird

---

9 **parasol**—*a small umbrella used to shield the sun*
10 **genially**—*in a friendly manner*
11 **permeated**—*spread through*

perched by his side was a bird of very different feather from those to which he was accustomed in his daily drives. He took his foot from the dashboard, pushed his hat back, and having thus cleared his mental decks for action, he took his first good look at the passenger, a look which she met with a grave, childlike stare of friendly curiosity.

Rebecca's eyes were like faith,—"the substance of things hoped for, the evidence of things not seen." Under her delicately etched brows they glowed like two stars, their dancing lights half hidden in lustrous darkness. Their glance was eager and full of interest, yet never satisfied; their steadfast gaze was brilliant and mysterious, and had the effect of looking directly through the obvious to something beyond, in the object, in the landscape, in you. They had never been accounted for, Rebecca's eyes. The school teacher and the minister at Temperance had tried and failed; the young artist who came for the summer to sketch the red barn, the ruined mill, and the bridge ended by giving up all these local beauties and devoting herself to the face of a child,—a small, plain face illuminated by a pair of eyes carrying such messages, such suggestions, such hints of sleeping power and insight, that one never tired of looking into their shining depths, nor of fancying that what one saw there was the reflection of one's own thought.

Mr. Cobb made none of these generalizations; his remark to his wife that night was simply to the effect that whenever the child looked at him she knocked him galley-west.[12]

---

[12] **knocked him galley-west**—*caused him to be confused*

"Miss Ross, a lady that paints, gave me the sun-shade," said Rebecca, when she had exchanged looks with Mr. Cobb and learned his face by heart. "Did you notice the pinked double ruffle and the white tip and handle? They're ivory. The handle is scarred, you see. That's because Fanny sucked and chewed it in meeting when I wasn't looking. I've never felt the same to Fanny since."

"Is Fanny your sister?"

"She's one of them."

"How many are there of you?"

"Seven. There's verses written about seven children:—

      " 'Quick was the little Maid's reply,
          O master! we are seven!'

I learned it to speak in school, but the scholars were hateful and laughed. Hannah is the oldest, I come next, then John, then Jenny, then Mark, then Fanny, then Mira."

"Well, that *is* a big family!"

"Far too big, everybody says," replied Rebecca. They're dear, but such a bother, and cost so much to feed, you see," she rippled on. "Hannah and I haven't done anything but put babies to bed at night and take them up in the morning for years and years. But it's finished, that's one comfort, and we'll have a lovely time when we're all grown up and the mortgage is paid off."

"All finished? Oh, you mean you've come away?"

"No, I mean they're all over and done with; our family's finished. Mother says so, and she always keeps her promises. There hasn't been any since Mira, and she's three. She was born the day father died. Aunt

Miranda wanted Hannah to come to Riverboro instead of me, but mother couldn't spare her; she takes hold of housework better than I do, Hannah does. I told mother last night if there was likely to be any more children while I was away I'd have to be sent for, for when there's a baby it always takes Hannah and me both, for mother has the cooking and the farm."

"Oh, you live on a farm, do ye? Where is it?—near to where you got on?"

"Near? Why, it must be thousands of miles! Our farm is away off from everywheres, but our school and meeting-house is at Temperance, and that's only two miles. Sitting up here with you is most as good as climbing the meeting-house steeple. I know a boy who's

been up on our steeple. He said the people and cows looked like flies. We haven't met any people yet, but I'm *kind* of disappointed in the cows;—they don't look so little as I hoped they would; still they don't look quite as big as if we were down side of them, do they? Boys always do the nice splendid things, and girls can only do the dull ones that get left over. They can't climb so high, or go so far, or stay out so late, or run so fast, or anything."

Mr. Cobb wiped his mouth on the back of his hand and gasped. He had a feeling that he was being hurried from peak to peak of a mountain range without time to take a good breath in between.

"I can't seem to locate your farm," he said, "though I've been to Temperance and used to live up that way. What's your folks' name?"

"Randall. My mother's name is Aurelia Randall; our names are Hannah Lucy Randall, Rebecca Rowena Randall, John Halifax Randall, Jenny Lind Randall, Marquis Randall, Fanny Ellsler Randall, and Miranda Randall. Mother named half of us and father the other half, but we didn't come out even, so they both thought it would be nice to name Mira after aunt Miranda in Riverboro; they hoped it might do some good, but it didn't, and now we call her Mira. We are all named after somebody in particular. I think that's all there is tell about us," she finished seriously.

"Land o' Liberty!" said Mr. Cobb. "There wa'n't many names left when your mother got through choosin'! You've got a powerful good memory! I guess it ain't no trouble for you to learn your lessons, is it?"

"Not much; the trouble is to get the shoes to go and learn 'em. These are spandy new I've got on, and they have to last six months. Mother always says to save my shoes. There don't seem to be any way of saving shoes but taking 'em off and going barefoot; but I can't do that in Riverboro without shaming Aunt Mirandy. I'm going to school right along now when I'm living with Aunt Mirandy, and in two years I'm going to the seminary at Wareham; mother says it ought to be the making of me! I'm going to be a painter like Miss Ross when I get through school. At any rate, that's what *I* think I'm going to be. Mother thinks I'd better teach."

"Your farm ain't the old Hobbs place, is it?"

"No, it's just Randall's Farm. At least that's what mother calls it. I call it Sunnybrook Farm."

"I guess it don't make no difference what you call it so long as you know where it is," remarked Mr. Cobb.

Rebecca turned the full light of her eyes upon him reproachfully, almost severely, as she answered:— "Oh! don't say that, and be like all the rest! It does make a difference what you call things. When I say Randall's Farm, do you see how it looks?"

"No, I can't say I do," responded Mr. Cobb uneasily.

"Now when I say Sunnybrook Farm, what does it make you think of?"

Mr. Cobb felt like a fish removed from his native[13] element and left panting on the sand; there was no evading the awful responsibility of a reply, for Rebecca's eyes were searchlights, that pierced the fiction of his brain and perceived the bald spot on the back of his head.

---

[13] **native**—*natural*

"I s'pose there's a brook somewheres near it," he said timorously.[14]

Rebecca looked disappointed but not quite disheartened. "That's pretty good," she said encouragingly. "You're warm but not hot; there's a brook, but not a common brook. It has young trees and baby bushes on each side of it, and it's a shallow chattering little brook with a white sandy bottom and lots of little shiny pebbles. Whenever there's a bit of sunshine the brook catches it, and it's always full of sparkles the livelong day. Don't your stomach feel hollow? Mine does! I was so 'fraid I'd miss the stage I couldn't eat any breakfast."

"You'd better have your lunch, then. I don't eat nothin' till I get to Milltown; then I get a piece o' pie and cup o' coffee. Now you watch me heave this newspaper right onto Mis' Brown's doorstep."

Piff! and the packet landed exactly as it was intended, on the corn husk mat in front of the screen door.

"Oh, how splendid that was!" cried Rebecca with enthusiasm. "Just like the knife thrower at the circus. I wish there was a long, long row of houses each with a corn husk mat and a screen door in the middle, and a newspaper to throw on every one!"

"I might fail on some of 'em, you know," said Mr. Cobb, beaming with modest pride. "There's the river again; this is the last long hill, and when we get to the top of it we'll see the chimbleys of Riverboro in the distance. 'Tain't fur. I live 'bout half a mile beyond the brick house myself."

Rebecca's hand stirred nervously in her lap and she moved in her seat. "I didn't think I was going to be

---

[14] **timorously**—*lacking in confidence*

afraid," she said almost under her breath; "but I guess I am, just a little mite—when you say it's coming so near."

"Would you go back?" asked Mr. Cobb curiously.

She flashed him an intrepid[15] look and then said proudly, "I'd never go back—I might be frightened, but I'd be ashamed to run. Is there a main street to the village, like that in Wareham?"

"I s'pose you might call it a main street, an' your aunt Sawyer lives on it, but there ain't no stores nor mills, an' it's an awful one-horse village! You have to go 'cross the river an' get on to our side if you want to see anything goin' on."

"I'm almost sorry," she sighed, "because it would be so grand to drive down a real main street, sitting high up like this behind two splendid horses, with my pink sunshade up, and everybody in town wondering who the bunch of lilacs and the hair trunk belongs to."

"There ain't no harm, as I can see, in our makin' the grand entry in the biggest style we can," said Mr. Cobb with a grin. "I'll set up straight, an' drive fast; you hold your bo'quet in your lap, an' open your little red parasol, an' we'll jest make the natives[16] stare!"

The child's face was radiant for a moment, but the glow faded just as quickly as she said, "I forgot—mother put me inside, and maybe she'd want me to be there when I got to aunt Mirandy's. Maybe I'd be more genteel inside, and then I wouldn't have to be jumped down and my clothes fly up, but could open the door and step down like a lady passenger. Would you please stop a minute, Mr. Cobb, and let me change?"

---

[15] intrepid—*fearless*
[16] natives—*those connected to a particular place by birth*

The stage driver good-naturedly pulled up his horses, lifted the excited little creature down, opened the door, and helped her in, putting the lilacs and the pink sunshade beside her.

"We've had a great trip," he said, "and we've got real well acquainted, haven't we?" Mr. Cobb said as he remounted his perch; and as the stage rumbled down the village street between the green maples, those who looked from their windows saw a little lady in buff calico sitting primly on the back seat holding a great bouquet tightly in one hand and a pink parasol in the other. Had they been farsighted enough they might have seen, when the stage turned into the side dooryard of the old brick house, a calico yoke[17] rising and falling tempestuously[18] over the beating heart beneath, the red color coming and going in two pale cheeks, and a mist of tears swimming in two brilliant dark eyes. Rebecca's journey had ended.

Riverboro, Rebecca's new home, might as well be a foreign country. The ways of her aunts—whom she barely knows—are nothing like the ways of her family at Sunnybrook. However, there are exciting opportunities in store for Rebecca. For the first time, she has the advantage of going to school regularly. And soon after her arrival, friendly, outgoing Rebecca makes a best friend for life. Although some of Rebecca's well-meaning efforts turn out to be disasters, she never loses heart. Readers have enjoyed this classic work of fiction for over one hundred years, and you will too.

---

[17] **yoke**—*part of a dress near the neck and shoulders*
[18] **tempestuously**—*forcefully*

Time to Think

1. Where was Rebecca going in the stagecoach?

2. Why did Rebecca ask to ride up front with Mr. Cobb rather than inside the coach?

3. How many children were in the Randall family? Explain how this chapter excerpt got its name.

4. Why did Rebecca call Randall's Farm Sunnybrook Farm?

I WONDER . . .

1. Which of these phrases from the story are examples of dialect?
   a. "O master! we are seven!"
   b. "'Tain't fur."
   c. "The old stagecoach was rumbling along the dusty road."
   d. "You can come up if you want to; there ain't no extry charge to sit side o' me."

2. What can you tell about the character of Rebecca from the way the author describes her?

3. In just a few pages, Rebecca has been revealed as a very lifelike character. Because this excerpt is from the beginning of a longer book, we cannot tell if Rebecca will grow and change or if she will remain the same throughout the book. What do you think? Explain your answer.

POETRY

Hi again! I've been working on my poetry lately, and one of the best ways to learn how to write poetry is to read it! Good poets use beautiful language; but more importantly, they give readers something to think about. The famous poet Gwendolyn Brooks did just that while she was a young girl.

At only thirteen years old, she published her first poem, "Eventide," and her first volume of poetry brought her into the spotlight. After winning the Pulitzer Prize in 1950, Gwendolyn Brooks went on to publish *Bronzeville Boys and Girls*, her first collection of poetry specifically for children. Gwendolyn dedicated the volume to her own children, who were also "Bronzeville boys and girls" growing up in the same Chicago neighborhood that had inspired their mother's poetry throughout her life.

Because Gwendolyn Brooks got her inspiration from the children in her neighborhood, she wrote about lifelike characters that share experiences with children everywhere. Each of the following poems has the name of a child in the title. Some are written as if the child were speaking about everyday themes like love, family, nature, and growing up. Because Gwendolyn Brooks wrote about childhood experiences, her poems are as meaningful today as they were when they were published nearly seventy years ago. Let's read a few.

219

Jim

Gwendolyn Brooks

There never was a nicer boy
Than Mrs. Jackson's Jim.
The sun should drop its greatest gold
On him.

Because, when Mother-dear was sick,
He brought her cocoa in.
And brought her broth, and brought her bread.
And brought her medicine.

And, tipping,* tidied up her room.
And would not let her see
He missed his game of baseball
Terribly.

* **tipping**—*tiptoeing*

Robert, Who Is Often a Stranger to Himself

Gwendolyn Brooks

Do you ever look in the looking-glass
And see a stranger there?
A child you know and do not know,
Wearing what you wear?

Cynthia
in the Snow
Gwendolyn Brooks

It SUSHES.
It hushes
The loudness in the road.
It flitter-twitters,
And laughs away from me.
It laughs a lovely whiteness,
And whitely whirs away,
To be
Some otherwhere,
Still white as milk or shirts.
So beautiful it hurts.

Marie Lucille
Gwendolyn Brooks

That clock is ticking
Me away!
The me that only
Yesterday
Ate peanuts, jam and
Licorice
Is gone already.
And this is
'Cause nothing's putting
Back, each day,
The me that clock is
Ticking away.

1. Which of Gwendolyn Brooks's poems follow the same rhyme scheme pattern?

2. Match each poem's title to its theme(s). Answers may be used more than once.

   "Cynthia in the Snow" •   • **family**

   "Jim" •   • **growing up**

   "Marie Lucille" •   • **love**

   **"Robert, Who Is Often
a Stranger to Himself"** •   • **nature**

3. Which two poems have a similar theme?

4. In "Marie Lucille," what did the poet mean by "The clock is ticking me away"?
   a. She is becoming smaller.
   b. She is changing over time.
   c. The day is getting shorter.

5. Can you relate to "Robert, Who Is Often a Stranger to Himself"? How is it possible to see yourself as a stranger in the mirror?

In Psalm 139:14, God's Word says, *"I will praise Thee; for I am fearfully and wonderfully made: marvellous are Thy works; and that my soul knoweth right well."* Sometimes the way a person actually looks does not match the picture they have of themselves in their mind. As we grow physically, we sometimes change very quickly, and it can be startling to see how we have changed.

In addition to the image that we see in the mirror, we are also bombarded with the images of others. Often it is suggested that this is the way we should look or act or dress. Once we start making comparisons, it is very easy to think that we do not measure up. Then we can too easily get caught up in trying to make ourselves into someone we are not. We can begin to feel discouraged and defeated if we allow ourselves to fall into that way of thinking.

Luke 2:52 tells us that even Jesus grew up physically just as each of us do. Hebrews tells us Jesus had the same human emotions that we all have, although He never sinned. Hebrews also tells us that He is filled with tender sympathy for us because He understands our feelings. Isn't it wonderful to know that He understands exactly who we are, and He loves us? Jesus is a friend we can rely on to help us think properly about ourselves and make wise decisions as we change and grow.

ELIZABETH ANN FAILS IN AN EXAMINATION

from *Understood Betsy*
by Dorothy Canfield Fisher

Ever since the death of her parents, Elizabeth Ann has been raised under the watchful care of Aunt Harriet and Aunt Frances. But when Aunt Harriet becomes ill, nine-year-old Elizabeth Ann must leave the only home she's ever known to live with other relatives—the Putney cousins. The Putneys— Uncle Henry, Aunt Abigail, and Cousin Ann—are very different from Aunt Frances. They are kind to Elizabeth Ann, but they do not dote on her as Aunt Frances used to. They expect her to do more on her own and to contribute to work on the farm. As Elizabeth Ann—or Betsy, as the Putneys call her—adjusts to her new life, she grows in ways she had never expected.

Something perfectly dreadful had happened in school that day. The Superintendent, the all-important, seldom-seen Superintendent, came to visit the school and the children were given some examinations so he could see how they were getting on.

Now, you know what an examination did to Elizabeth Ann. Or haven't I told you yet?

Well, if I haven't, it's because words fail me. If there is anything horrid that an examination *did*n't do to Elizabeth Ann, I have yet to hear of it. It began years ago, before ever she went to school, when she heard Aunt Frances talking about how *she* had dreaded exami- nations when she was a child, and how they dried up her mouth and made her ears ring and her head ache and her knees get all weak and her mind a perfect blank, so that she didn't know what two and two made. Of course Elizabeth Ann didn't feel *all* those things right off at her first examination, but by the time she had had several and had rushed to tell Aunt Frances about how awful they were and the two of them had sympathized with one another and compared symptoms and then wept about her resulting low marks, why, she not only had all the symptoms Aunt Frances had ever had, but a good many more of her own invention.

Well, she had had them all and had them hard this afternoon, when the Superintendent was there. Her mouth had gone dry and her knees had shaken and her elbows had felt as though they had no more bones in them than so much jelly, and her eyes had smarted,[1] and oh, what answers she had made! That dreadful tight panic had clutched at her throat whenever the

---

[1] smarted—*hurt*

Superintendent had looked at her, and she had disgraced herself ten times over. She went hot and cold to think of it, and felt quite sick with hurt vanity. She who did so well every day and was so much looked up to by her classmates, what *must* they be thinking of her! To tell the truth, she had been crying as she walked along through the woods, because she was so sorry for herself. Her eyes were all red still, and her throat sore from the big lump in it.

And now she would live it all over again as she told the Putney cousins. For of course they must be told. She had always told Aunt Frances everything that happened in school. It happened that Aunt Abigail had been taking a nap when she got home from school, and so she had come out to the sap house, where Cousin Ann and Uncle Henry were making syrup, to have it over with as soon as possible. She went up to the little slab house now, dragging her feet and hanging her head, and opened the door.

Cousin Ann, in an old skirt and a work coat and high rubber boots, was just poking some more wood into the big fire which blazed furiously under the broad, flat pan where the sap was boiling. The rough, brown hut was filled with white steam and the sweetest of all odors, hot maple syrup. Cousin Ann turned her head, her face red with the heat of the fire, and nodded at the child.

"Hello, Betsy, you're just in time. I've saved out a cupful of hot syrup for you, all ready to wax."

Betsy hardly heard this, although she had been wild about waxed sugar on snow ever since her very first taste of it. "Cousin Ann," she said unhappily, "the Superintendent visited our school this afternoon."

"Did he?" said Cousin Ann, dipping a thermometer into the boiling syrup.

"Yes, and we had *examinations*!" said Betsy.

"Did you?" said Cousin Ann, holding the thermometer up to the light and looking at it.

"And you know how perfectly awful examinations make you feel," said Betsy, very near to tears again.

"Why, no," said Cousin Ann, sorting over syrup tins. "They never made me feel awful. I thought they were sort of fun."

"*Fun!*" cried Betsy, indignantly,[2] staring through the beginnings of her tears.

"Why, yes. Like taking a dare, don't you know. Somebody stumps you to jump off the hitching post, and you do it to show 'em. I always used to think examinations were like that. Somebody stumps you to spell 'pneumonia,' and you do it to show 'em. Here's

---

[2] **indignantly**—*angrily as if offended*

your cup of syrup. You'd better go right out and wax it while it's hot."

Elizabeth Ann automatically took the cup in her hand, but she did not look at it. "But supposing you get so scared you can't spell 'pneumonia' or anything else!" she said feelingly. "That's what happened to me. You know how your mouth gets all dry and your knees. . . ." She stopped. Cousin Ann had said she did *not* know all about those things. "Well, anyhow, I got so scared I could hardly stand *up*! And I made the most awful mistakes—things I know just as *well*! I spelled 'doubt' without any 'b' and 'separate' with an 'e,' and I said Iowa was bounded on the north by *Wisconsin*, and I . . ."

"Oh, well," said Cousin Ann, "it doesn't matter if you really know the right answers, does it? That's the important thing."

This was an idea which had never in all her life entered Betsy's brain and she did not take it in now. She only shook her head miserably and went on in a doleful[3] tone. "And I said 13 and 8 are *22*! and I wrote March without any capital M, and I . . ."

"Look here, Betsy, do you *want* to tell me all this?" Cousin Ann spoke in the quick, ringing voice she had once in a while which made everybody open his eyes and get his wits about him. Betsy gathered hers and thought hard; and she came to an unexpected conclusion. No, she didn't really want to tell Cousin Ann all about it. Why was she doing it? Because she thought that was the thing to do. "Because if you don't really want to," went on Cousin Ann, "I don't see that it's doing anybody any good. I guess Hemlock Mountain will

---

[3] **doleful**—*full of grief and sadness*

stand right there just the same even if you did forget to put a 'b' in 'doubt.' And your syrup will be too cool to wax right if you don't take it out pretty soon."

She turned to stoke the fire, and Elizabeth Ann, in a daze, found herself walking out of the door. It fell shut after her, and there she was under the clear, pale-blue sky, with the sun just hovering over the rim of Hemlock Mountain. She looked up at the big mountains, all blue and silver with shadows and snow, and wondered what in the world Cousin Ann had meant. Of course Hemlock Mountain would stand there just the same. But what of it? What did that have to do with her arithmetic, with anything? She had failed in her examination, hadn't she?

She found a clean white snowbank under a pine tree, and setting her cup of syrup down in a safe place, began to pat the snow down hard to make the right bed for the waxing of the syrup. The sun, very hot for that late March day, brought out strongly the tarry perfume[4] of the big pine tree. Near her the sap dripped musically into a bucket, already half full, hung on a maple tree. A bluejay rushed suddenly through the upper branches of the wood, his screaming and chattering voice sounding like noisy children at play.

Elizabeth Ann took up her cup and poured some of the thick, hot syrup out on the hard snow, making loops and curves as she poured. It stiffened and hardened at once, and she lifted up a great coil of it, threw her head back, and let it drop into her mouth. Concentrated sweetness of summer days was in that mouthful, part of it still hot and aromatic, part of it icy and wet with melting snow. She crunched it all together into a delicious

---

[4] **tarry perfume**—*scent of pine tar*

big lump and sucked on it dreamily, her eyes on the rim of Hemlock Mountain, high above her there, the snow on it bright golden in the sunlight. Uncle Henry had promised to take her up to the top as soon as the snow went off. She wondered what the top of a mountain would be like. Uncle Henry had said the main thing was that you could see so much of the world at once. He said it was so strange the way your own house and big barn and great fields looked like little toy things that weren't of any account. It was because you could see so much more than just the . . .

She heard an imploring whine, and a cold nose was thrust into her hand! Why, there was old Shep begging for his share of waxed sugar. He loved it, though it did stick to his teeth so! She poured out another lot and gave half of it to Shep. It immediately stuck his jaws together tight, and he began pawing at his mouth and shaking his head till Betsy had to laugh. Then he managed to pull his jaws apart and chewed loudly and visibly, tossing his head, opening his mouth wide till Betsy could see the sticky, brown candy draped in melting festoons[5] all over his big white teeth and red gullet.[6] Then with a gulp he had swallowed it all down and was whining for more, striking softly at the little girl's skirt with his paw. "Oh, you eat it too fast!" cried Betsy, but she shared her next lot with him too. The sun had gone down over Hemlock Mountain by this time, and the big slope above her was all deep blue shadow. Betsy ate the last of her sugar, looking up at the quiet giant there, towering grandly above her. There was no lump in her throat now. Although she still thought she did not know what in the

[5] **festoons**—*strings of decoration*
[6] **gullet**—*throat*

world Cousin Ann meant by saying that about Hemlock Mountain and her examination, it's my opinion that she had made a good beginning of an understanding.

She was just picking up her cup to take it back to the sap house when Shep growled a little and stood with his ears and tail up, looking down the road. Something was coming down that road in the blue, clear twilight, something that was making a very strange noise. It sounded almost like somebody crying. It *was* somebody crying! It was a child crying. It was a little, little girl. . . . Betsy could see her now . . . stumbling along and crying as though her heart would break. Why, it was little Molly, her own particular charge at school, whose reading lesson she heard every day. Besty and Shep ran to meet her. "What's the matter, Molly? What's the matter?" Betsy knelt down and put her arms around the weeping child. "Did you fall down? Did you hurt yourself? What are you doing 'way off here? Did you lose your way?"

"I don't want to go away! I don't want to go away!" said Molly over and over, clinging tightly to Betsy. It was a long time before Betsy could quiet her enough to find out what had happened. Then she made out between Molly's sobs that her mother had been taken suddenly sick and had to go away to a hospital, and that left nobody at home to take care of Molly, and she was to be sent away to some strange relatives in the city who didn't want her to come and who said so right out. . . .

Elizabeth Ann knew all about that! Her heart swelled big with sympathy. She knew that ghastly[7] feeling of being unwanted. She knew why little Molly was crying! And she shut her hands together hard and made up her mind that she *would* help her out!

Do you know what she did, right off, without thinking about it? She didn't go and look up Aunt Abigail. She didn't wait 'til Uncle Henry came back from his round of emptying sap buckets into the big tub on his sled. As fast as her feet could carry her she flew back to Cousin Ann in the sap house. I can't tell you (except again that Cousin Ann was Cousin Ann) why it was that Betsy ran so fast to her and was so sure that everything would be all right as soon as Cousin Ann knew about it; but whatever the reason was it was a good one, for, though Cousin Ann did not stop to kiss Molly or even to look at her more than one sharp first glance, she said after a moment's pause, during which she filled a syrup can and screwed the cover down very tight: "Well, if her folks will let her stay, how would you like to have Molly come and stay with us 'til her mother gets back

---

[7] **ghastly**—*terrible*

234

from the hospital? Now you've got a room of your own, I guess if you wanted to you could have her sleep with you."

"Oh, Molly, Molly, *Molly!*" shouted Betsy, jumping up and down, and then hugging the little girl with all her might. "Oh, it will be like having a little sister!"

Cousin Ann sounded a dry, warning note: "Don't be too sure her folks will let her. We don't know about them yet."

Betsy ran to her, and caught her hand, looking up at her with shining eyes. "Cousin Ann, if *you* go to see them and ask them, they will!"

This made even Cousin Ann give a little abashed[8] smile of pleasure, although she made her face grave again at once and said: "You'd better go along back to the house now, Betsy. It's time for you to help Mother with the supper."

The two children trotted back along the darkening wood road, Shep running before them, little Molly clinging fast to the older child's hand. "Aren't you ever afraid, Betsy, in the woods this way?" she asked admiringly, looking about her with timid eyes.

"Oh, no!" said Betsy, protectingly, "there's nothing to be afraid of, except getting off on the wrong fork of the road, near the Wolf Pit."

"Oh, *ow!*" said Molly scringing.[9] "What's the Wolf Pit? What an awful name!"

Betsy laughed. She tried to make her laugh sound brave like Cousin Ann's, which always seemed so scornful of being afraid. As a matter of fact, she was beginning to fear that they *had* made the wrong turn, and she

---

[8] **abashed**—*ashamed; embarrassed*
[9] **scringing**—*cringing*

was not quite sure that she could find the way home. But she put this out of her mind and walked along very fast, peering ahead into the dusk. "It hasn't anything to do with wolves," she said in answer to Molly's question, "anyhow, not now. It's just a big, deep hole in the ground where a brook had dug out a cave. . . . Uncle Henry told me all about it when he showed it to me . . . and then part of the roof caved in; sometimes there's ice in the corner of the covered part all the summer, Aunt Abigail says."

"Why do you call it the Wolf Pit?" asked Molly, walking very close to Betsy and holding very tightly to her hand.

"Oh, long, ever so long ago, when the first settlers came up here, they heard a wolf howling all night, and when it didn't stop in the morning, they came up here on the mountain and found a wolf had fallen in and couldn't get out."

"My! I hope they killed him!" said Molly.

"Gracious! That was more than a hundred years ago," said Betsy. She was not thinking of what she was saying. She was thinking that if they *were* on the right road they ought to be home by this time. She was thinking that the right road ran downhill to the house all the way, and that this certainly seemed to be going up a little. She was wondering what had become of Shep. "Stand here just a minute, Molly," she said. "I want . . . I just want to go ahead a little bit and see . . . and see. . . ." She darted on around a curve of the road and stood still, her heart sinking. The road turned there and led straight up the mountain!

For just a moment the little girl felt a wild impulse to burst out in a shriek for Aunt Frances, and to run crazily away, anywhere so long as she was running. But the thought of Molly standing back there, trustfully waiting to be taken care of, shut Betsy's lips together hard before her scream of fright got out. She stood still, thinking. Now she mustn't get frightened. All they had to do was to walk back along the road till they came to the fork and then make the right turn. But what if they didn't get back to the turn 'til it was so dark they couldn't see it? . . . Well, she mustn't think of that. She ran back, calling, "Come on, Molly," in a tone she tried to make as firm as Cousin Ann's. "I guess we have made the wrong turn after all. We'd better . . ."

But there was no Molly there. In the brief moment Betsy had stood thinking, Molly had disappeared. The long, shadowy wood road held not a trace of her.

Then Betsy was frightened and then she *did* begin to scream, at the top of her voice, "Molly! Molly!" She was beside herself with terror, and started back hastily to hear Molly's voice, very faint, apparently coming from the ground under her feet.

"Ow! Ow! Betsy! Get me out! Get me out!"

"Where *are* you?" shrieked Betsy.

"I don't know!" came Molly's sobbing voice. "I just moved the least little bit out of the road, and slipped on the ice and began to slide and I couldn't stop myself and I fell down into a deep hole!"

Betsy's head felt as though her hair was standing up straight on end with horror. Molly must have fallen down into the Wolf Pit! Yes, they were quite near it.

She remembered now that big white-birch tree stood right at the place where the brook tumbled over the edge and fell into it. Although she was dreadfully afraid of falling in herself, she went cautiously over to this tree, feeling her way with her foot to make sure she did not slip, and peered down into the cavernous gloom below. Yes, there was Molly's little face, just a white speck. The child was crying, sobbing, and holding up her arms to Betsy.

"Are you hurt, Molly?"

"No. I fell into a big snowbank, but I'm all wet and frozen and I want to get out! I want to get out!"

Betsy held on to the birch tree. Her head whirled. What *should* she do! "Look here, Molly," she called down, "I'm going to run back along to the right road and back to the house and get Uncle Henry. He'll come with a rope and get you out!"

At this Molly's crying rose to a frantic scream. "Oh, Betsy, don't leave me here alone! Don't! Don't! The wolves will get me! Betsy, *don't* leave me alone!" The child was wild with terror.

"But I *can't* get you out myself!" screamed back Betsy, crying herself. Her teeth were chattering with the cold.

"Don't go! Don't go!" came up from the darkness of the pit in a piteous howl. Betsy made a great effort and stopped crying. She sat down on a stone and tried to think. And this is what came into her mind as a guide: "What would Cousin Ann do if she were here? She wouldn't cry. She would *think* of something."

Betsy looked around her desperately. The first thing she saw was the big limb of a pine tree, broken off by the wind, which half lay and half slantingly stood up against a tree a little distance above the mouth of the pit. It had been there so long that the needles had dried and fallen off, and the skeleton of the branch with the broken stubs looked like . . . yes, it looked like a ladder! *That* was what Cousin Ann would have done!

"Wait a minute! Wait a minute, Molly!" she called wildly down the pit, warm all over in excitement. "Now listen. You go off there in a corner, where the ground makes a sort of roof. I'm going to throw down something you can climb up on, maybe."

"Ow! Ow, it'll hit me!" cried poor little Molly, more and more frightened. But she scrambled off under her shelter obediently, while Betsy struggled with the branch. It was so firmly imbedded in the snow that at first she could not budge it at all. But after she cleared that away and pried[10] hard with the stick she was using as a lever she felt it give a little. She bore down with all her might, throwing her weight again and again on her lever, and finally felt the big branch move. After that it was easier, as its course was downhill over the snow to the mouth of the pit. Glowing and pushing, wet with perspiration, she slowly maneuvered it along to the edge, turned it squarely, gave it a great shove, and leaned over anxiously. Then she gave a great sigh of relief! Just as she had hoped, it went down sharp end first and stuck fast in the snow which had saved Molly from broken bones. She was so out of breath with her work that for a moment she could not speak. Then, "Molly, there! Now I guess you can climb up to where I can reach you."

---

[10] **pried**—*forced open with a lever*

Molly made a rush for any way out of her prison, and climbed, like the practiced squirrel that she was, up from one stub to another to the top of the branch. She was still below the edge of the pit there, but Betsy lay flat down on the snow and held out her hands. Molly took hold hard, and, digging her toes into the snow, slowly wormed her way up to the surface of the ground.

It was then, at that very moment, that Shep came bounding up to them, barking loudly, and after him Cousin Ann striding along in her rubber boots, with a lantern in her hand and a rather anxious look on her face.

She stopped short and looked at the two little girls, covered with snow, their faces flaming with excitement, and at the black hole gaping behind them. "I always *told* Father we ought to put a fence around that pit," she said in a matter-of-fact voice. "Some day a sheep's going to fall down there. Shep came along to the house without you, and we thought most likely you'd taken the wrong turn."

Betsy felt terribly aggrieved.[11] She wanted to be praised for heroism. She wanted Cousin Ann to *realize* . . . oh, if Aunt Frances were only there, *she* would realize! . . .

"I fell down in the hole, and Betsy wanted to go and get Mr. Putney, but I wouldn't let her, and so she threw down a big branch and I climbed out," explained Molly, who, now that her danger was past, took Betsy's action quite as a matter of course.

"Oh, that was how it happened," said Cousin Ann. She looked down the hole and saw the big branch, and looked back and saw the long trail of crushed snow where Betsy had dragged it. "Well, now, that was quite a good idea for a little girl to have," she said briefly. "I guess you'll do to take care of Molly all right!"

She spoke in her usual voice and immediately drew the children after her, but Betsy's heart was singing joyfully as she trotted along clasping Cousin Ann's strong hand. Now she knew that Cousin Ann realized. . . . She trotted fast, smiling to herself in the darkness.

"What made you think of doing that?" asked Cousin Ann presently, as they approached the house.

"Why, I tried to think what *you* would have done if you'd been there," said Betsy.

"Oh!" said Cousin Ann. "Well . . ."

---

[11] **aggrieved**—*offended*

She didn't say another word, but Betsy, glancing up into her face as they stepped into the lighted room, saw an expression that made her give a little skip and hop of joy. She had *pleased* Cousin Ann.

That night, as she lay in her bed, her arm over Molly cuddled up warm beside her, she remembered, ever so faintly, as something of no importance, that she had failed in an examination that afternoon.

Before Elizabeth Ann came to live with the Putneys, she had never done anything for herself. Although she was nine years old, she had never fixed her own hair—she had never even hung up her own coat. She has come a long way since that first day in Vermont, and as she experiences a very different sort of life at Putney Farm and in the village school, she has become more and more confident. When she is faced with a challenge that would have caused the old Elizabeth Ann to be petrified with fear, the new Betsy thinks on her feet and rises to the occasion. Then a letter arrives unexpectedly, and Betsy must make a difficult choice. Will she go back to being the Elizabeth Ann she used to be, or will she continue to grow into the Betsy she is becoming?

Understood Betsy was written in 1916, and some of the things Betsy and other children of that time experienced are no longer typical of our lives today. However, the themes of learning, growth, and independence are as true as ever, making this book an enduring and enjoyable classic.

Time to Think

1. Why had Elizabeth Ann had a terrible day at school?

2. What details does the author use to show Elizabeth Ann's emotion during the examination? What emotion was she experiencing?

3. What was Cousin Ann's reaction to Elizabeth Ann's failure?

4. Why had Molly come crying to Betsy?

5. Betsy reacts very differently to situations than Cousin Ann does. Each reacted differently to Molly's dilemma. How did Betsy react? How did Cousin Ann react? Explain your answer.

6. How did Betsy rescue Molly from the "Wolf Pit"? What character traits does Betsy show with this solution?

7. How does the final paragraph show Betsy's growth?

I WONDER . . .

Write a few of your favorite descriptive phrases written by Dorothy Canfield Fischer.

Was Betsy right to feel "aggrieved" that Cousin Ann didn't praise her for rescuing Molly? Was her reaction natural? All of us like to be praised. Praise that comes from another person whom we love or respect can be very meaningful to us. It is one way we know that what we have done pleases them. But how do we respond when we don't receive praise? Are we hurt? Do we feel as if something we deserve has been withheld?

Because of the way Elizabeth Ann had been brought up, she always looked to her Aunt Frances for approval and praise. However, the Putneys showed their love and approval in a very different way. After Betsy rescued Molly from the "Wolf Pit," Cousin Ann responded in her typical matter-of-fact way. Betsy's first reaction was to feel offended. Betsy expected that a big fuss should have been made; after all, she had been unusually brave and quick-thinking. Before the story ended, Betsy did come to realize that Cousin Ann showed her approval differently than Aunt Frances had.

Sometimes, though, the praise we think we deserve never does come. What should our attitude be then? Colossians 3:22–24 tells us. Although this passage is specifically addressed to servants, the principle is there for us all to follow. We are urged to obey because all that a Christian does is ultimately in service to the Lord Jesus. We do what is right not to be seen of others and earn their praise; we do it *"heartily, as to the Lord, and not unto men."* Someday we may receive His highest praise, *"Well done, thou good and faithful servant"* (Matthew 25:21).

To make Sugar Wax, see pages 280–281.

from Genesis 37

¹ And Jacob dwelt in the land wherein his father was a stranger, in the land of Canaan. ² These are the generations of Jacob. Joseph, being seventeen years old, was feeding the flock with his brethren; and the lad was with the sons of Bilhah, and with the sons of Zilpah, his father's wives: and Joseph brought unto his father their evil report. ³ Now Israel loved Joseph more than all his children, because he was the son of his old age: and he made him a coat of many colours. ⁴ And when his brethren saw that their father loved him more than all his brethren, they hated him, and could not speak peaceably unto him. ⁵ And Joseph dreamed a dream, and he told it his brethren: and they hated him yet the more.

¹² And his brethren went to feed their father's flock in Shechem. ¹³ And Israel said unto Joseph, Do not thy brethren feed the flock in Shechem? come, and I will send thee unto them. And he said to him, Here am I. ¹⁴ And he said to him, Go, I pray thee, see whether it be well with thy brethren, and well with the flocks; and bring me word again. So he sent him out of the vale of Hebron, and he came to Shechem. ¹⁵ And a certain man found him, and, behold, he was wandering in the field: and the man asked him, saying, What seekest thou? ¹⁶ And he said, I seek my brethren: tell me, I pray thee, where they feed their flocks.

¹⁷ And the man said, They are departed hence; for I heard them say, Let us go to Dothan. And Joseph went after his brethren, and found them in Dothan. ¹⁸ And when they saw him afar off, even before he came near unto them, they conspired against him to slay him. ¹⁹ And they said one to another, Behold, this dreamer cometh. ²⁰ Come now therefore, and let us slay him, and cast him into some pit, and we will say, Some evil beast hath devoured him: and we shall see what will become of his dreams.

²⁶ And Judah said unto his brethren, What profit is it if we slay our brother, and conceal his blood? ²⁷ Come, and let us sell him to the Ishmaelites, and let not our hand be upon him; for he is our brother and our flesh. And his brethren were content.
²⁸ Then there passed by Midianites merchantmen; and they drew and lifted up Joseph out of the pit, and sold Joseph to the Ishmaelites for twenty pieces of silver: and they brought Joseph into Egypt.

³⁶ And the Midianites sold him into Egypt unto Potiphar, an officer of Pharaoh's, and captain of the guard.

Time to Think

1. Which of the following describes this selection? Explain the difference.
   a. narrative fiction   b. scriptural account

2. What special gift was given to Joseph, and who was it from?

3. How did Joseph's brothers respond to the favor Jacob (Israel) showed to Joseph?

4. What errand was Joseph sent to do?

5. When Joseph's brothers saw him coming, what was the plan they devised?

6. For what reason was Joseph's life spared?

THINK ON THESE THINGS

Joseph's brothers, the children of Israel, became bitter when their father showed favoritism toward Joseph. Although there may have been reason for their hurt, there was no excuse for their actions. How do you think these unresolved feelings will affect their lives and the lives of others?

Hebrews 12:15 warns us about what can happen if we harbor bitterness in our hearts toward others. But it also gives us the key to handle this difficult emotion.

> *"Looking diligently lest any man fail of the grace of God; lest any root of bitterness springing up trouble you, and thereby many be defiled."*

What is the warning? What is the key?

MEANT FOR GOOD

Jennifer Odom

Becoming a house servant in the palace of Joseph, the vizier[1] of Egypt, to pay his family's debt was not in Jabare's plans for his future. Surprisingly, Jabare will discover that his story is similar to Joseph's. While both have suffered unfair experiences, Joseph seems to be more at peace than Jabare. Why is that? What is the difference between Joseph and Jabare? As we read this fictional story with a setting based on biblical events in the life of Joseph, we will see that often the things that seem bad in our lives are meant for good when we trust in God.

Jabare could not believe his father's words. He knew the heavy burden his father carried, but he never thought it would come to this. Jabare's head spun with the news—he was to be sold as a servant! Jabare knew

---

[1] **vizier**—*the position in which Joseph served in Egypt; second-in-command under Pharaoh*

other Egyptian families had needed to make the same choice, but he never imagined this outcome for himself.

Even now his father's words echoed in his heart. "My son," his father had said sorrowfully, "I have worked and saved to pay our taxes to Pharaoh, but it has not been enough. The only option I have left is to place you as a servant to pay off our debt. You are eleven years old, strong and energetic; and I have taught you the value of hard work. I know you will give the house of your father a good name."

Jabare was unsure how to feel about this new responsibility. His father had been told Jabare would be placed as a house servant in the palace of Joseph, the vizier of Egypt. While this was a desirable position, Jabare did not understand why he had to give up his life and dreams to pay the family debt. Many of his friends were planning for their futures and homes of their own.

Now, at this important time in his life, he was being forced into servanthood to pay off a debt that was not his! Where was the justice in that? Oh, he knew his father would have never wanted this. It hurt Jabare to see the sorrow in his father's eyes. He knew his father had done all he could, but the famine had begun and was predicted to last seven years. Pharaoh had plenty. Could he not forgive this debt of his father's and allow Jabare to go on with his life as planned?

The next day, as Jabare stood before the door of the vizier's palace, his heart beat hard in his chest. He had told his family goodbye that morning. He already felt the homesickness settling in as he tried to keep up his courage here at Joseph's palace. Over were the cozy nights, sitting at a meal with Mother, Father, and his nine-year-old sister, Neferet. He would be able to see them from time to time, but he would no longer live at home. Although Jabare's father had reminded him that his name meant bravery, he felt anything but brave! As the great door opened and Jabare stepped inside, a seed of bitterness began to grow within him toward the great Pharaoh.

𓏢 𓂋𓃭𓆓𓂝 𓂋𓏏𓆑𓃭𓆓𓏏 𓂋𓏏𓆣 𓏏𓃀𓏤

The next few weeks were spent in training for his duties in Joseph's home. He was to be one of the young servants who brought food and drink to the vizier and his guests. It was an important position, and Jabare knew it was considered a privilege. Perhaps others felt that way, but Jabare had plans for his future. This "privilege" was not a part of the plan! With each day, Jabare became more bitter. He did his job, but he would never consider it a privilege!

The famine brought new challenges almost daily as Joseph accepted guests from both near and far. The vizier was different from Egyptian men. Jabare had heard he was from a foreign country. The vizier dressed and looked like an Egyptian, but he worshipped a God unknown to the Egyptian people. Jabare had been told Joseph gave his God credit for the ability to interpret Pharaoh's dream. The dream had been a vision telling of the famine to come. After Joseph had interpreted Pharaoh's dream, Pharaoh placed him second-in-command of the land of Egypt. Joseph had spent the seven years of plenty gathering food to last through the next seven years of famine. Jabare did not know if Joseph's God existed, but he knew the vizier had been wise to prepare Egypt for these desperate days of famine.

On the days Jabare was able to go and visit his family, he often saw the friends his age he had once spent his days with as a boy. Now, three years later, the same old friends were establishing their own jobs and homes. At fourteen years of age, Egyptian boys were treated as men. He loved his visits back home, but each time the bitterness grew a little deeper. What good could possibly come from all of this?

As Jabare brought food and drink to Joseph, he often was asked to stay in the room and continue to serve the vizier and his guests. Foreigners came almost daily now, hoping to purchase food from the Egyptian storerooms. In order to do so, they must first have an audience with the vizier.

Jabare stood in the palace room where Joseph accepted his guests. It was like any other ordinary day; desperate people needing food for their families came to Joseph for help. Suddenly, Jabare noticed an obvious difference in Joseph's reaction. A group of ten men walked into the room. Sent by their father, they had traveled a long way to buy food for their households. As the men stood before the vizier, he spoke harshly to them, much to Jabare's surprise. Joseph was not known as a harsh ruler; but, instead, he was kind and gracious.

Jabare heard Joseph say to the men, "Where do you come from?"

The brothers answered, "From the land of Canaan to buy food."

After a short pause in which Joseph seemed to be studying them, he said, "You are spies! You have come to see our barren land!" Jabare's interest was piqued[2] at the mention of possible spies.

"No, my lord, only to buy food. We are all one man's sons; we are true men; we are no spies."

Joseph once more said, "No, you have come to see the famine in our land." The room became quiet, and the uneasiness increased as time seemed to stand still. Could these men possibly be spies as Joseph had said?

Trembling, the brothers answered, "Your servants are twelve brothers, the sons of one man in the land of Canaan; the youngest is this day with our father, and the other one is dead."

In a threatening tone that Jabare had never heard Joseph use before, he said to the brothers, "No! I have spoken truly. You are spies! You'll have to prove to me that you are not. You will stay in my prison while one

---

[2] **piqued**—*created a curiosity within*

of you goes back for the younger brother. Until you prove yourselves, you are surely spies!"

Jabare watched in astonishment as guards took the ten men and put them in prison. The men didn't seem dangerous, but Joseph must have known something about them that Jabare did not. Three days later, Joseph called for the men to be brought up from the prison. As they stood before him, Joseph said, "Do what I say, and you will all live; for I fear God. If you are telling the truth, leave one brother here while the rest of you return to your home. Take corn for your families, but bring your youngest brother to me. Then I will know that you were truthful, and you will not die."

The brothers began to talk among themselves. Joseph had been speaking through an interpreter. The men did not realize he could understand what they were saying to one another. Jabare had learned some Hebrew from Joseph and could also understand the brothers. He heard one of them say, "We are truly guilty concerning our brother, in that we saw how fearful he was when he begged us, and we would not hear; this is why we are in trouble now." The oldest brother, Reuben, told the brothers, "Did I not tell you, 'Do not sin against the child'; and you would not listen? We must pay for his death!'"

As they spoke, Jabare noticed that Joseph was overcome with what appeared to be great sorrow. He watched the vizier hide himself from the brothers. Joseph seemed to be weeping, but why? What would cause the vizier to react in such a way to the story the brothers told of their deceased brother? A few moments passed in which the brothers did not notice Joseph's reaction. He returned, calm and steady once more. He took the brother named

Simeon, bound him in chains in front of them, and sent the men to prepare for their journey home.

While the brothers prepared for their trip, Joseph commanded the servants in the room to secretly return the men's money to their bags of food. He also gave them the food they would need for their trip. One moment, Joseph was accusing them of being spies; the next, he was giving them their money back. What a strange day this had been! Jabare helped put the money in the sacks of corn. As he handled the bags of money, he thought of his father. If Pharaoh could afford to give away this much corn and provisions, why couldn't he forgive his father's debt? Jabare's bitterness grew a little more as he watched the brothers start on their journey.

Jabare's days were busy, and he forgot about the ten men and their visit to Egypt. He spent his days in the palace with Joseph. He watched him as he met with those who came for help. Jabare often heard his master speak of his God. Joseph talked of how God gave great wisdom to those who asked. Joseph prayed before making decisions, asking Him to guide his thoughts. Jabare could sense a deep relationship between Joseph and his God. Of course, Jabare was unable to ask the vizier questions, but he was curious. Why did Joseph seem to rely on his God so greatly? The Egyptian gods Jabare had known never seemed to listen or do much for him. In the middle of the bitterness that had grown in his young heart, Jabare began to experience a small flame of desire to know more about this God that Joseph loved and worshipped.

254

One especially hot and dry day, word passed quickly among the servants that the brothers from Canaan had returned. The palace was busy preparing a feast Joseph had requested. The ten brothers had brought their younger brother with them. Joseph told the ruler of his household to bring the men to his home and prepare the finest of meals. He wanted them to dine with him at noon. As Jabare watched the men enter the room where the feast was prepared, he could sense their fear.

Jabare overheard their conversation as the brothers waited for Joseph to join them. "Because of the money that was returned in our sacks at the first time we came, we might all become his slaves!" When the ruler of Joseph's house approached the men, they began explaining how money had been found in their sacks when they returned home. They assured the ruler they had returned with their money and brought even more money to buy more food. Their fear and nervousness grew as they talked. With a smile, the ruler answered, "Be at peace. Fear not: Your God, and your father's God has provided for you; I had your money."

Before leading them to the table for the feast with Joseph, the ruler of the house brought Simeon from the prison. Jabare watched as the men hugged one another and thanked their God for keeping Simeon safe. Their prayers and worship were the same as Joseph offered to his God.

The men prepared for the meal by washing their feet and gathering the gifts they had brought for Joseph. Jabare stood very still, almost holding his breath, as he waited for the vizier to enter the room. He wondered if the brothers would be treated as spies once again.

When Joseph entered the room, the brothers presented him with gifts and bowed themselves to the ground.

Joseph asked the brothers if their father was still alive. Jabare thought it odd that Joseph would care so much about someone he had never seen. The brothers assured Joseph that their father Israel was well. Joseph then fixed his gaze on the youngest brother, Benjamin. The whole room grew silent as Joseph seemed to be studying the boy. Quietly, Joseph asked, "Is this your younger brother?" Looking at Benjamin he tenderly said, "God be gracious unto thee, my son."

Day after day, Jabare had watched Joseph receive guests. Never had he seen Joseph act in any way other than a strong leader. Joseph stood firm no matter what came his way, praying to his God for wisdom. Jabare watched Joseph, overcome with emotion, retreat quickly to his chambers. Jabare had come to respect and even to love the vizier. He was aware their country would be suffering hunger without the hard work and preparation of Joseph. Jabare wondered if Joseph's God would bring the comfort Joseph needed.

At Joseph's abrupt exit from the room, the brothers were puzzled. Why had this Egyptian ruler grown sorrowful after seeing their younger brother? In just a few moments, Joseph returned to the room and ordered the meal to begin. Everyone sat down, and Jabare began serving the vizier and his guests. After the meal, Joseph ordered the ruler of the house to fill the brothers' sacks with food and put their money back in the sack again. Stranger still, Jabare was asked to place Joseph's own cup in the sack of the youngest brother.

The next morning, the brothers left, heading home to their father. Having arrived early at the palace to begin his day, Jabare heard Joseph tell the steward[3] of the house to go after the brothers, to look through their bags, and ask why they had stolen from the vizier. The steward left immediately and in a short time returned with the brothers. Of course, the brothers had no idea how Joseph's cup and their money had been found in their sacks. They were fearful of how the vizier would respond.

"What have you done?" asked Joseph of the brothers. Judah responded, "What do you want us to say? How can we prove our innocence? God knows our past sins. We will stay and become servants in your house." Joseph answered, "God forbid that I would do this. The one whose sack contains my cup will be my servant. The rest of you will go in peace back to your father."

---

[3] **steward**—*a person in charge of the daily operations of another's household, finances, business, etc.*

Judah stepped forward and asked to speak to Joseph privately. As the two men talked, Jabare noticed that the look on his master's face was not angry, but tender. As Judah continued, he reminded Joseph of their father who was old and unwilling to allow his youngest son to travel with them. He was the only one left alive of two sons born of his mother. Jabare listened as Judah continued to explain to Joseph about his father's great sadness over his son who had died. Then Judah offered himself as a servant in place of his brother Benjamin.

Jabare closely watched his master as he spoke. Jabare had grown to respect the vizier. Day after day he had observed Joseph help those who came to him; he listened to him pray to his God for wisdom and guidance. As the brother pleaded with Joseph, Jabare thought he sensed a change in Joseph, but why?

Without warning, Joseph began to weep loudly. He had lost the ability to hide the emotion Jabare had seen growing as Judah spoke. Joseph cried out, "Make every man to leave the room!" All the servants, astonished and quiet, left the room, but Joseph's weeping could still be heard outside the door.

They listened as Joseph revealed to the brothers, "I am Joseph your brother; does my father still live?" Silence permeated[4] the room as the brothers contemplated[5] the words of Joseph. "Come near to me," Joseph said to the men. The brothers hesitantly stepped closer to the vizier. "I am Joseph your brother, whom you sold into Egypt."

---

[4] **permeated**—*to spread throughout completely*
[5] **contemplated**—*thought about for a lengthy time*

Jabare's mind began to race. The vizier had been sold into Egypt as a slave? By his own brothers? Joseph went on, "Do not be angry with yourselves because you sold me into slavery. I know that God had a specific purpose for my life. It was God Who sent me to Egypt, made me a ruler over the land, and enabled me to save the lives of many during this famine. You meant it for evil, but our God meant it for good."

As Jabare listened outside the door, he began to understand that Joseph's life had taken a different course than Joseph had once expected. Jabare felt he understood the vizier a little more—they had similar stories. Jabare couldn't help but wonder how Joseph was able to faithfully worship his God Who sent him to Egypt as a slave. A few days later, Jabare visited his family and felt he wanted to talk through these thoughts with his father.

"I can't really explain what happened in the palace, Father. Joseph's revealing himself to his brothers was like nothing I have ever witnessed before. The vizier feels it is his God Who is responsible for the hardship he has faced. Yet, he still speaks of Him with great worship, thanking Him for all He has done in his life. I just don't understand!"

Jabare's father listened carefully. He could sense his son's deep struggle. "Father, I am beginning to believe that Joseph's God is the true God. If Joseph loves and trusts his God Who sent him to Egypt as a slave, there must be something real about Joseph's God. Joseph believes that although his brothers meant to do him evil, his God meant it for good."

As Jabare continued his work in the palace, his admiration for Joseph grew, along with his faith in Joseph's God. Jabare wanted Joseph's God to be his God. Jabare's own life had been changed against his will. Perhaps the God of Joseph could also turn his life around for good. "God of Joseph," Jabare prayed in the quiet of his own room, "Take my life and make it for good as You have Joseph's. I put all my trust in You. Please help me to see that Your way and plan for my life is only ever good."

If you would like to read about how God cared for Joseph and the children of Israel, the biblical account of this portion of the life of Joseph can be found in *Genesis 45–50*.

Time to Think

1. Which of the following describes this selection? Explain your answer.
   a. narrative fiction   b. scriptural account

2. As the story began, what upsetting news did Jabare learn?

3. Whose house was Jabare a servant in?

4. Why was there a lack of provisions in the land?

5. What did Jabare's name mean? Why did his father remind him of this?

6. What accusation was made against the brothers from Canaan?

7. After watching Joseph in his position as vizier, how did Jabare feel toward Joseph?

8. What did Jabare see in Joseph's behavior that made him curious about Joseph's God?

I WONDER . . .

1. What did Jabare tell his father he was beginning to believe?

2. What decisions did Jabare make that were influenced by Joseph's example?

3. What did Jabare ask God to allow him to understand and see?

4. What is the theme of the story?

How can our actions influence those around us, especially those who may not know Christ?

People around you hear what you say and see what you do. If you have siblings, you know just how true this is! When you love Jesus and want to please Him, you also want to represent Him well before others. You have the opportunity to influence those around you, for good or for bad. We can see from the Bible record that Joseph set a good example before others. In the New Testament, Paul encouraged young Timothy to be an example as well (1 Timothy 4:12).

Although it is your responsibility to represent Christ well before others, the outcome is not in your hands. Some people will be influenced for good; some will ignore your good testimony; some may even make fun of you when you want to do right. The ultimate outcome is in God's hands. He reminds us in Scripture that His thoughts are not our thoughts (Isaiah 55:8–9). We could attempt to understand all of His ways, but that is beyond our capabilities as human beings (Romans 11:33). It is up to us to do right and leave the results to Him.

from Genesis 45–50

Genesis 45

¹ Then Joseph could not refrain himself before all them that stood by him; and he cried, Cause every man to go out from me. And there stood no man with him, while Joseph made himself known unto his brethren. ² And he wept aloud: and the Egyptians and the house of Pharaoh heard. ³ And Joseph said unto his brethren, I am Joseph; doth my father yet live? And his brethren could not answer him; for they were troubled at his presence.

⁴ And Joseph said unto his brethren, Come near to me, I pray you. And they came near. And he said, I am Joseph your brother, whom ye sold into Egypt. ⁵ Now therefore be not grieved, nor angry with yourselves, that ye sold me hither: for God did send me before you to preserve life.

⁹ Haste ye, and go up to my father, and say unto him, Thus saith thy son Joseph, God hath made me lord of all Egypt: come down unto me, tarry not: ¹⁰ and thou shalt dwell in the land of Goshen, and thou shalt be near unto me, thou, and thy children, and thy children's children, and thy flocks, and thy herds, and all that thou hast: ¹¹ and there will I nourish thee; for yet there are five years of famine; lest thou, and thy household, and all that thou hast, come to poverty.

Genesis 48

¹ And it came to pass after these things, that one told Joseph, Behold, thy father is sick: and he took with him his two sons, Manasseh and Ephraim. ² And one told Jacob, and said, Behold, thy son Joseph cometh unto thee: and Israel strengthened

himself, and sat upon the bed. ³ And Jacob said unto Joseph, God Almighty appeared unto me at Luz in the land of Canaan, and blessed me, ⁴ and said unto me, Behold, I will make thee fruitful, and multiply thee, and I will make of thee a multitude of people; and will give this land to thy seed after thee for an everlasting possession. ⁵ And now thy two sons, Ephraim and Manasseh, which were born unto thee in the land of Egypt before I came unto thee into Egypt, are mine; as Reuben and Simeon, they shall be mine.

Genesis 49

³³ And when Jacob had made an end of commanding his sons, he gathered up his feet into the bed, and yielded up the ghost, and was gathered unto his people.

Genesis 50

¹⁵ And when Joseph's brethren saw that their father was dead, they said, Joseph will peradventure hate us, and will certainly requite us all the evil which we did unto him. ¹⁶ And they sent a messenger unto Joseph, saying, Thy father did command before he died, saying, ¹⁷ So shall ye say unto Joseph, Forgive, I pray thee now, the trespass of thy brethren, and their sin; for they did unto thee evil: and now, we pray thee, forgive the trespass of the servants of the God of thy father. And Joseph wept when they spake unto him. ¹⁸ And his brethren also went and fell down before his face; and they said, Behold, we be thy servants. ¹⁹ And Joseph said unto them, Fear not: for am I in the place of God? ²⁰ But as for you, ye thought evil against me; but God meant it unto good, to bring to pass, as it is this day, to save much people alive.

Time to Think

1. What news did Joseph reveal to his brothers?

2. According to Joseph, for what reason did God send him to Egypt?

3. What plan did Joseph have for caring for his father and brothers during the famine?

4. Before Jacob died, what did he tell Joseph about Joseph's two sons?

5. What did Joseph's brothers fear after Jacob died?

6. What was Joseph's reaction when his brothers asked for forgiveness and mercy?

I W O N D E R . . .

1. How does the fictional narrative "Meant for Good" differ from the scriptural accounts you read from Genesis?

2. Name some clues in "Meant for Good" that tell you the narrative is fictional.

THINK ON THESE THINGS

"But I say unto you, Love your enemies, bless them that curse you, do good to them that hate you, and pray for them which despitefully use you, and persecute you." —Matthew 5:44

Joseph's brothers had not treated him kindly. Yet, even after all they did to him, Joseph still cared for their needs during the famine. What lessons can we learn from Joseph's example?

SAMUEL'S SCRIPT

THE FINAL BOW

I don't know about you, but I have some new favorite characters after reading *In Character*! It's been a lot of fun to see how the authors developed each of the characters in their stories.

In "The Case of the Poetic Pranks," Lucas changed from a boy detective who wanted to get all the credit to one who was a team player and recognized the others for their ability.

Then, there was the way Jay Berry told about his adventures in *Summer of the Monkeys*. His storytelling reminded me of some of the funny stories my grandfather has told me about his childhood.

266

And speaking of my grandfather, here's something else he told me.

"Samuel," he said. "Do you know you are developing your own character? I don't mean like a character in a story. I mean your own character—the real you—the part of you that can demonstrate traits like responsibility, kindness, honesty, and hard work—the kind of character God wants you to have."

I hadn't really thought about it; but sometimes, when I read about people in history or the people in the Bible and their character, I wonder if I will *ever* be what God wants me to be.

After reading about Jabare and the life of Joseph, I can see that God works through bad choices, difficult circumstances, and even sinful actions to help us learn to be more like Him. Although Joseph's family lacked the character traits to make good choices, God patiently worked in their lives and helped them to see their weaknesses. Each character grew and changed, and God used it all for good.

I am beginning to understand that as I grow up, I will learn more about God's plan for me; and I pray that God will help me develop my character to be more and more like His.

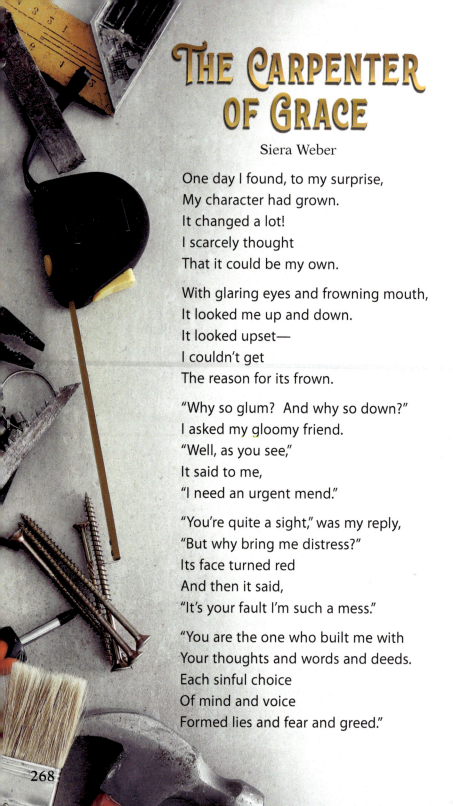

THE CARPENTER OF GRACE

Siera Weber

One day I found, to my surprise,
My character had grown.
It changed a lot!
I scarcely thought
That it could be my own.

With glaring eyes and frowning mouth,
It looked me up and down.
It looked upset—
I couldn't get
The reason for its frown.

"Why so glum? And why so down?"
I asked my gloomy friend.
"Well, as you see,"
It said to me,
"I need an urgent mend."

"You're quite a sight," was my reply,
"But why bring me distress?"
Its face turned red
And then it said,
"It's your fault I'm such a mess."

"You are the one who built me with
Your thoughts and words and deeds.
Each sinful choice
Of mind and voice
Formed lies and fear and greed."

"Oh no!" I cried. "What will we do?"
Our case seemed rather bleak.
"Oh, do not fret—
There's still hope yet:
A Carpenter to seek."

This Carpenter began at once—
He sawed, sanded, mended.
It hurt a bit,
But I'll admit,
The results were truly splendid.

At times, the choices that I make
Still mar my old friend's face.
But now I know
To Whom I'll go—
My Carpenter of Grace.

 *Time to Think*

1. What first built the narrator's character?

2. Why do you think the narrator was surprised by how his character had changed?

3. Why did the Carpenter's work "hurt a bit"?

 THINK ON THESE THINGS

Who is the Carpenter of Grace? Explain the meaning of His name.

Psalm 51:10 says, *"Create in me a clean heart, O God; and renew a right spirit within me."* When we are willing for God to make us clean and we ask Him to do it, He will.

ANALYZING THE MAIN CHARACTER

Complete after "Rufus and the Fatal Four" on page 4.

Identify the main character. Fill in the blanks describing his thoughts, feelings, actions, and physical characteristics. Choose one main character trait to describe him.

Thoughts

Main Character

Feelings

Actions

Main Character Trait

Physical Characteristics

❖ SUMMARIZE THE PLOT ❖

Complete after "The Peterkins Snowed-Up" on page 35.

Summarize what happened at the beginning, middle, and end.

Beginning _____

_____

_____

_____

_____

_____

Middle _____

_____

_____

_____

_____

_____

_____

End _____

_____

_____

_____

_____

_____

_____

_____

271

EXAMINE
⟐ NARRATIVE TEXT STRUCTURE ⟐

Complete after "Beezus and Her Little Sister" on page 52.

Using the numbers and letters provided, match each character and each plot detail with the correct setting. Some characters will be used more than once. "Ramona's Home" is done for you.

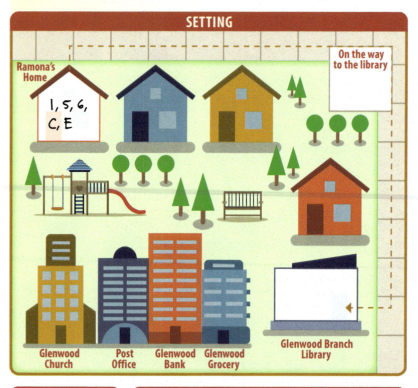

SETTING

Ramona's Home

1, 5, 6, C, E

On the way to the library

Glenwood Church   Post Office   Glenwood Bank   Glenwood Grocery   Glenwood Branch Library

CHARACTERS

1. Beezus
2. Miss Evans
3. Miss Greever
4. Mrs. Wisser
5. Mother
6. Ramona

PLOT

A. a character showed off her scab and bunny ears

B. a character needed to sign her name but was unable to

C. a book was written in

D. a book was purchased

E. one character began to understand another

ANALYZE
CHARACTER DEVELOPMENT

Complete after the excerpt from *The Hundred Dresses* on page 74.

Classify each of the following characters: Peggy, Maddie, Wanda, Jake, and the teacher. Remember that some characters will fit into more than one classification. Describe each character.

How are these characters lifelike?

Multi-dimensional

One-dimensional

Stays the Same

The Hundred Dresses

What is their single characteristic?

Grows and Changes

How do they change and grow?

CREATIVE COLLABORATION

Complete after *Castle Confusion* on page 102.

Collaborate to put on the play *Castle Confusion*. Decide who will be in charge of directing, scenery, cast members, props, and costumes. Select a cast and summarize the story to create a playbill on pp. 275, 276. Create a set of a medieval castle including scenery, props, and costumes. Perform the staged play before an audience. Don't forget to thank the adults who helped you.

Notes: _____

_____

_____

_____

List the props and costumes. _____

_____

_____

_____

_____

_____

Sketch the set.

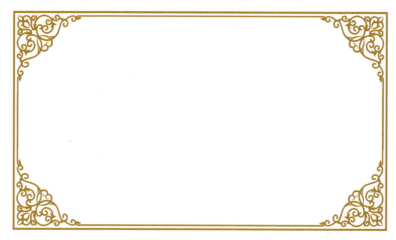

274

Castle Confusion

THE CAST OF CHARACTERS
(in order of appearance)

Lord Philip _____

King Edwin _____

Lady Jane _____

Jester _____

Lord Geoffrey _____

Lady Isabel _____

Queen Cecelia _____

Lady Charlotte _____

Production Staff and Crew

director   **scenery**   **cast**

_____ _____ _____

props   **costumes**

_____ _____

Summary
ACT 1

_____

_____

_____

_____

_____

_____

(cont.)

CREATIVE COLLABORATION (cont.)

ACT 2

ACT 3

Special Thanks

PLAN AND WRITE A MYSTERY

Complete after "Samuel's Script" on page 142.

Write your own mystery: choose your characters and crime.
Plan clues and distracters from beginning to end. Using your
plan, write your own mystery on a separate sheet of paper.

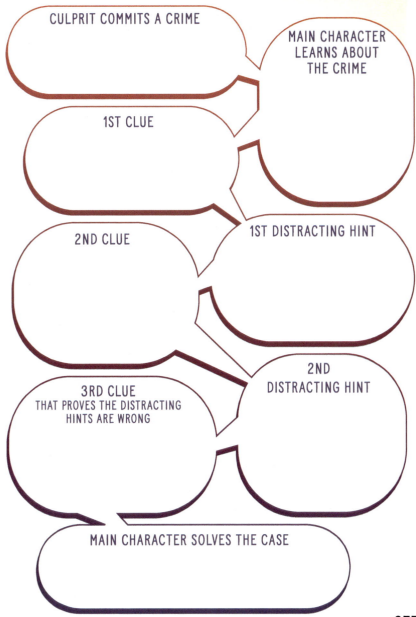

CULPRIT COMMITS A CRIME

MAIN CHARACTER
LEARNS ABOUT
THE CRIME

1ST CLUE

2ND CLUE

1ST DISTRACTING HINT

3RD CLUE
THAT PROVES THE DISTRACTING
HINTS ARE WRONG

2ND
DISTRACTING HINT

MAIN CHARACTER SOLVES THE CASE

COMPARE AND CONTRAST
❖ CHARACTERS ❖

Complete after *Hans Brinker, or the Silver Skates* on page 170.

Compare and contrast the traits of Peggy from *The Hundred Dresses* and Hilda from *Hans Brinker, or the Silver Skates*.

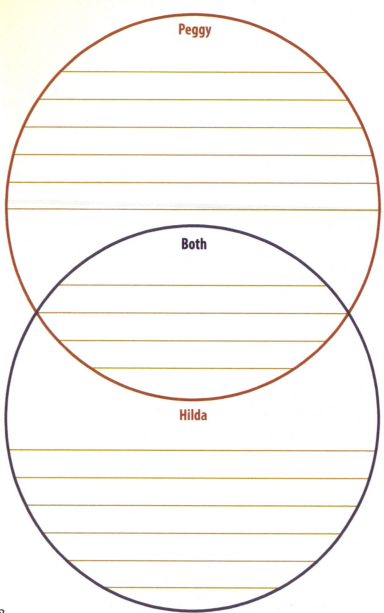

ANALYZE
❧ THE MAIN CHARACTER ❧

Complete after "Pippi Finds a Snirkle" on page 184.

List the main character's traits and provide proof of the trait from the text along with the page number where the proof was found. The first one is done for you.

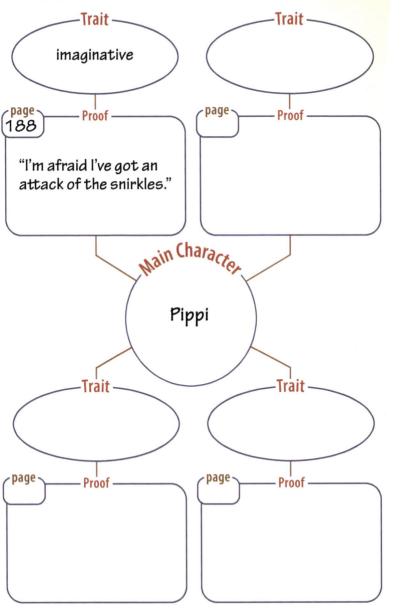

Trait

imaginative

page 188

Proof

"I'm afraid I've got an attack of the snirkles."

Trait

page

Proof

Main Character

Pippi

Trait

page

Proof

Trait

page

Proof

❖ Make Sugar Wax ❖

Complete after "Elizabeth Ann Fails an Examination" on page 226.

Did your mouth water as the author described the sugar wax that Betsy enjoyed? This treat—which is also called sugar on snow or jack wax—is traditional wherever maple syrup is made. However, you do not need to have your own maple trees and sap house in order to make it. Pure maple syrup purchased at the store works just as well. (Other kinds of syrup will not produce the same result.) Ask for the help of an adult to make this delicious candy.

Equipment

- 9" x 13" metal baking pan
- small metal saucepan with a heavy bottom
- candy thermometer
- heatproof measuring cup or small pitcher
- fork for each person (You may also use craft sticks.)

Ingredients

- clean snow (If snow is not available, substitute shaved or very finely crushed ice.)
- 1 cup of pure maple syrup

Directions

1. Pack the snow very firmly into the baking pan. It must be kept very cold. If it is cold enough outside, you may set the pan in a safe place outside until you are ready to use it.

2. Pour the maple syrup into the saucepan and clip the candy thermometer to the side of the pan, making sure it does not touch the bottom of the pan. Heat the syrup over medium-low heat until it boils.

3. Once the syrup boils, lower the temperature slightly and allow the syrup to bubble gently until it reaches the temperature of 230°F. This usually takes about 20 minutes. It is important to watch it constantly.

4. Pour the hot syrup into the heat-resistant measuring cup or pitcher.

5. Retrieve the pan of snow and slowly pour the hot syrup back and forth over the snow, making "ribbons."

6. Pick up a ribbon of candy, using a fork or stick to wrap it up.

7. Enjoy your sweet treat! Since it does not keep well, you will want to eat it all very soon.

   Optional: If you want to follow a very old tradition, serve sour pickles and donuts on the side.

 Time to Think

1. What are some other names for sugar wax?

2. What will happen if you do not use pure maple syrup?

3. What is the purpose of the candy thermometer?

 I WONDER . . .

1. Why do you think the pan of snow is prepared before the syrup is heated?

2. How important is it that the steps are followed in order?

CREDITS